Nginx 1 Web Server Implementation Cookbook

Over 100 recipes to master using the Nginx HTTP server and reverse proxy

Dipankar Sarkar

BIRMINGHAM - MUMBAI

Nginx 1 Web Server Implementation Cookbook

First published: May 2011

Production Reference: 1180511

Published by Packt Publishing Ltd.
32 Lincoln Road
Olton
Birmingham, B27 6PA, UK.

ISBN 978-1-849514-96-5

www.packtpub.com

Cover Image by Javier Barria (jbarriac@yahoo.com)

Credits

Author

Dipankar Sarkar

Reviewers

Valery Kholodkov

José Miguel Parrella

Michael Shadle

Acquisition Editor

Usha Iyer

Development Editor

Hyacintha D'Souza

Technical Editor

Kavita Iyer

Copy Editor

Neha Shetty

Project Coordinator

Srimoyee Ghoshal

Proofreader

Samantha Lyon

Indexer

Tejal Daruwale

Graphics

Nilesh Mohite

Production Coordinator

Kruthika Dangera

Cover Work

Kruthika Bangera

About the Author

Dipankar Sarkar is a web and mobile entrepreneur. He has a Bachelor's degree in Computer Science and Engineering from the Indian Institute of Technology, Delhi. He is a firm believer in the Open source movement and has participated in the Google Summer of Code, 2005-06 and 2006-07. He has conducted technical workshops for Windows mobile and Python at various technical meet ups. He recently took part in the Startup Leadership Program, Delhi Chapter.

He has worked with Slideshare LLC, one of the world's largest online presentation hosting and sharing service as an early engineering employee. He has since then worked with Mpower Mobile LLC, a mobile payment startup and Clickable LLC, a leading search engine marketing startup. He was a co-founder at Kwippy, which was one of the top micro-blogging sites. He is currently working in the social TV space and has co-founded Jaja.

This is his first technical publication

I would like to thank my patient and long suffering wife, Maitrayee, for putting up with my insane working hours and for being there for me throughout. My mother and my sister, Rickta and Amrita, whose belief and support sustains me. My in laws, Amal and Ruchira Roychoudhury, for opening their homes and hearts to me so generously. Also to my father, the late A. C. Sarkar, who co-authored the first chapter of my life and without whom none of this would have been possible.

I would also like to thank Usha, Hyacintha, Srimoyee, and Kavita from Packt who made this opportunity possible and have been fantastic to work with. I am deeply grateful to the technical reviewers whose insights have been invaluable. Needless to say, errors, if any, are mine.

About the Reviewers

Valery Kholodkov is an active member of Nginx community and one of the earliest module developers for Nginx. He's been a computer enthusiast since the age of 10 and has solid experience in developing scalable web applications and realtime control systems.

Valery helps people with scaling their websites. He has worked for various companies whose business depends on how fast their website is and how many requests servers can process within reasonable amount of time. In his blog "Nginx Guts" he writes about the internals of Nginx web server and shares his best practices in Nginx.

José Miguel is a Venezuelan IT professional based in Quito, Ecuador. Passionate about technology since the age of three, he started working with Linux servers in 2002, and he started working as a lead for a Linux deployment at a Venezuelan Government office (SAPI) in 2004, at the age of 17.

Afterwards he became an advisor and private consultant on Linux and open source software architecture and deployment for organizations such as the National Oil Company (PDVSA) as well as the IT/Telecom Regulators, National Phone Company, National Library, and other institutions in Venezuela as well as Ecuador and the US.

He also held a position as a datacenter analyst for EDELCA, one of the largest hydro power utilities worldwide, where he developed several system clusters with Nginx as well as the desktop Debian-based distribution. This experience led José Miguel to be the architect of Canaima 2.0, the national Linux distribution in Venezuela and now a community project, currently topping 1 million installations in a 1:1 school laptop project as well as State-funded computers.

In 2008 he accepted the position of Country Manager for ONUVA in Ecuador, one of the most renowned open source consulting firms in South America, altogether with the Chief Technology Officer position. While in ONUVA he had the opportunity to lead a team of professionals in Venezuela, Ecuador, and the US in large IT projects. Since 2010 he's been working as an open source strategy lead for a software development company.

José Miguel continues to be involved in technology communities worldwide, such as the Debian Project, where he's part of the Nginx maintenance team, but also the LACNIC Security Group, some Perl Mongers chapters, and local Linux User Groups. He's been an international speaker at venues such as Argentina, México, Scotland, and India and continues to devote some time to technical writing and presentations on his blog.

Michael Shadle is a self-proclaimed surgeon when it comes to procedural PHP. He has been using PHP for over ten years along with MySQL and various Linux and BSD distributions. He has used many different web servers over the years and considers Nginx to be the best solution yet.

During the day he works as a senior Web Developer at Intel Corporation on a handful of public-facing websites. He enjoys using his breadth of knowledge to come up with "out-of-the-box" solutions to solve the variety of issues and requests that come up. During his off-hours, he has a thriving personal consulting and web development practice and more personal project ideas than he can tackle at once.

He is a minimalist at heart, and believes that when architecting solutions, starting small and simple allows for a more agile approach in the long run. Michael also coined the phrase "A simple stack is a happy stack."

You can visit his personal blog at `http://michaelshadle.com/`.

I'd like to thank my parents, my friends, and the thousands of people I've interacted with over the Internet for keeping me on my toes.

www.PacktPub.com

Support files, eBooks, discount offers and more

You might want to visit www.PacktPub.com for support files and downloads related to your book.

Did you know that Packt offers eBook versions of every book published, with PDF and ePub files available? You can upgrade to the eBook version at www.PacktPub.com and as a print book customer, you are entitled to a discount on the eBook copy. Get in touch with us at service@packtpub.com for more details.

At www.PacktPub.com, you can also read a collection of free technical articles, sign up for a range of free newsletters and receive exclusive discounts and offers on Packt books and eBooks.

http://PacktLib.PacktPub.com

Do you need instant solutions to your IT questions? PacktLib is Packt's online digital book library. Here, you can access, read and search across Packt's entire library of books.

Why Subscribe?

- ► Fully searchable across every book published by Packt
- ► Copy and paste, print and bookmark content
- ► On demand and accessible via web browser

Free Access for Packt account holders

If you have an account with Packt at www.PacktPub.com, you can use this to access PacktLib today and view nine entirely free books. Simply use your login credentials for immediate access.

Table of Contents

Preface

Nginx is an open source high-performance web server, which has gained quite some popularity recently. Due to its modular architecture and small footprint, it has been the default choice for a lot of smaller Web 2.0 companies to be used as a load-balancing proxy server. It supports most of the existing backend web protocols such as FCGI, WSGI, and SCGI. This book is for you if you want to have in-depth knowledge of the Nginx server.

Nginx 1 Web Server Implementation Cookbook covers the whole range of techniques that would prove useful for you in setting up a very effective web application with the Nginx web server. It has recipes for lesser-known applications of Nginx like a mail proxy server, streaming of video files, image resizing on the fly, and much more.

The first chapter of the book covers the basics that would be useful for anyone who is starting with Nginx. Each recipe is designed to be independent of the others.

The book has recipes based on broad areas such as core, logging, rewrites, security, and others. We look at ways to optimize your Nginx setup, setting up your WordPress blog, blocking bots that post spam on your site, setting up monitoring using munin, and much more.

Nginx 1 Web Server Implementation Cookbook makes your entry into the Nginx world easy with step-by-step recipes for nearly all the tasks necessary to run your own web application.

A practical guide for system administrators and web developers alike to get the best out of the open source Nginx web server.

What this book covers

Chapter 1, The Core HTTP Module, deals with the basics of Nginx configuration and implementation. By the end of it you should be able to compile Nginx on your machine, create virtual hosts, set up user tracking, and get PHP to work.

Chapter 2, All About Rewrites: The Rewrite Module, is devoted to the rewrite module; it will teach you the basics and also allow you to configure various commonly available web development frameworks to work correctly with your Nginx setup using the correct rewrite rules.

Chapter 3, Get It All Logged: The Logging Module, aims to teach the basics as well as the advanced configurations that can be done around the Nginx logging module, like log management, backup, rotation, and more. Logging is very crucial as it can help you identify and track various attributes of your application like performance, user behavior, and much more. It also helps you as a system administrator to identify, both reactively and proactively, potential security issues.

Chapter 4, Slow Them Down: Access and Rate Limiting Module, explains how Nginx provides good protection against cases such as bringing down sites by providing rate limiting and server access based on IP.

Chapter 5, Let's be Secure: Security Modules, looks at how we can use the security modules built-in Nginx to secure your site and user's data.

Chapter 6, Setting Up Applications: FCGI and WSGI Modules, has a practical section devoted to helping programmers and system administrators understand and install their applications using Nginx as the web server. Due to the lack of integrated modules for running PHP and Python, the setting up of such systems can be an issue for non-experienced system administrators.

Chapter 7, Nginx as a Reverse Proxy, deals with the usage of Nginx as a reverse proxy in various common scenarios. We will have a look at how we can set up a rail application; set up load balancing, and also have a look at caching setup using Nginx, which will potentially enhance the performance of your existing site without any codebase changes.

Chapter 8, Improving Performance and SEO Using Nginx, is all about how you can make your site load faster and possibly get more traffic on your site. We will cover the basics of optimizing your Nginx setup and some SEO tricks. These techniques will not only be useful for your SEO, but also for the overall health of your site and applications.

Chapter 9, Using Other Third-party Modules, a look at some inbuilt and third-party modules which allow us to extend and use Nginx with other protocols such as IMAP, POP3, WebDAV, and much more. Due to the flexible and well-defined module API, many module developers have used Nginx for interesting web-based tasks such as XSLT transformations, image resizing, and HTTP publish-subscribe server.

Chapter 10, Some More Third-party Modules, looks at various web situations such as load balancing, server health checks, and more which will be very useful in a production environment. These simple recipes will be highly applicable in enterprise scenarios where you may need to have analytics, external authentication schemes, and many other situations.

What you need for this book

In terms of understanding, a bit of web server administration experience would help. If you understand how a basic site works, it would be easier to follow some of the more production oriented configurations. A look at the index of recipes would give you a good overview of the topics and also show some of the connectivity throughout the book at a glace.

All the code in this book has been tried and tested on the following software setup

1. Ubuntu/debian linux with 2.6.x kernel

2. Nginx 0.7.x+ to 1.0.0

3. Installed compiler dependencies for Nginx

Nginx binaries are available for windows as well, compiling the modules however will be easier to by using cygwin based setups.

Some patience and reading maybe required to make more effective use of what you can do with the learnings in the book. Have fun 'Nginx'ing !

Who this book is for

If you are tired of Apache consuming all your server memory with little traffic, and to overcome this, or for some other reason, you are looking for a high-performance load-balancing proxy server and have tried using Nginx, then this book is for you. You need some basic knowledge of Nginx. System administrators and web developers will benefit greatly from this book.

Conventions

In this book, you will find a number of styles of text that distinguish between different kinds of information. Here are some examples of these styles, and an explanation of their meaning.

Code words in text are shown as follows: "We can include other contexts through the use of the include directive."

A block of code is set as follows:

```
int main()
{
    // Open the video file
    cv::VideoCapture capture("../bike.avi");
    // check if video successfully opened
    if (!capture.isOpened())
        return 1;
```

When we wish to draw your attention to a particular part of a code block, the relevant lines or items are set in bold:

```
    server 192.168.1.3;
    server 192.168.1.5;
    fair;
}
server {
```

Any command-line input or output is written as follows:

```
/etc/init.d/nginx restart
```

New terms and **important words** are shown in bold. Words that you see on the screen, in menus or dialog boxes for example, appear in the text like this: "clicking the **Next** button moves you to the next screen".

> Warnings or important notes appear in a box like this.

> Tips and tricks appear like this.

Reader feedback

Feedback from our readers is always welcome. Let us know what you think about this book—what you liked or may have disliked. Reader feedback is important for us to develop titles that you really get the most out of.

To send us general feedback, simply send an e-mail to feedback@packtpub.com, and mention the book title via the subject of your message.

If there is a book that you need and would like to see us publish, please send us a note in the **SUGGEST A TITLE** form on www.packtpub.com or e-mail suggest@packtpub.com.

If there is a topic that you have expertise in and you are interested in either writing or contributing to a book, see our author guide on www.packtpub.com/authors.

Customer support

Now that you are the proud owner of a Packt book, we have a number of things to help you to get the most from your purchase.

Downloading the example code

You can download the example code files for all Packt books you have purchased from your account at http://www.PacktPub.com. If you purchased this book elsewhere, you can visit http://www.PacktPub.com/support and register to have the files e-mailed directly to you.

Errata

Although we have taken every care to ensure the accuracy of our content, mistakes do happen. If you find a mistake in one of our books—maybe a mistake in the text or the code—we would be grateful if you would report this to us. By doing so, you can save other readers from frustration and help us improve subsequent versions of this book. If you find any errata, please report them by visiting http://www.packtpub.com/support, selecting your book, clicking on the **errata submission form** link, and entering the details of your errata. Once your errata are verified, your submission will be accepted and the errata will be uploaded on our website, or added to any list of existing errata, under the Errata section of that title. Any existing errata can be viewed by selecting your title from http://www.packtpub.com/support.

Piracy

Piracy of copyright material on the Internet is an ongoing problem across all media. At Packt, we take the protection of our copyright and licenses very seriously. If you come across any illegal copies of our works, in any form, on the Internet, please provide us with the location address or website name immediately so that we can pursue a remedy.

Please contact us at copyright@packtpub.com with a link to the suspected pirated material.

We appreciate your help in protecting our authors, and our ability to bring you valuable content.

Questions

You can contact us at questions@packtpub.com if you are having a problem with any aspect of the book, and we will do our best to address it.

1
The Core HTTP Module

In this chapter, we will cover:

- ▶ Installing new modules and compiling Nginx
- ▶ Running Nginx in debug mode
- ▶ Easy reloading of Nginx using the CLI
- ▶ Splitting configuration files for better management
- ▶ Setting up multiple virtual hosts
- ▶ Setting up a default catch-all virtual host
- ▶ Using wildcards in virtual hosts
- ▶ Setting up the number of worker processes correctly
- ▶ Increasing the size of uploaded files
- ▶ Using dynamic SSI for simple sites
- ▶ Adding content before and after a particular page
- ▶ Enabling auto indexing of a directory
- ▶ Serving any random web page from a directory
- ▶ Serving cookies for identifying and logging users
- ▶ Re-encoding the response to another encoding
- ▶ Enabling Gzip compression on some content types
- ▶ Setting up 404 and other error pages

Introduction

This chapter deals with the basics of Nginx configuration and implementation. By the end of it you should be able to compile Nginx on your machine, create virtual hosts, set up user tracking, and get PHP to work.

Installing new modules and compiling Nginx

Today, most softwares are designed to be modular and extensible. Nginx, with its great community, has an amazing set of modules out there that lets it do some pretty interesting things. Although most operating system distributions have Nginx binaries in their repositories, it is a necessary skill to be able to compile new, bleeding edge modules, and try them out. Now we will outline how one can go about compiling and installing Nginx with its numerous third-party modules.

How to do it...

1. The first step is to get the latest Nginx distribution, so that you are in sync with the security and performance patches (`http://sysoev.ru/nginx/nginx-0.7.67.tar.gz`). Do note that you will require sudo or root access to do some of the installation steps going ahead.

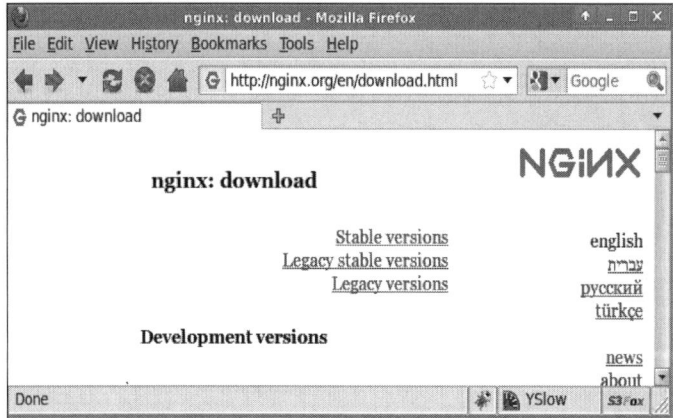

2. Un-tar the Nginx source code. This is simple, you will need to enter the following command:

```
tar -xvzf nginx-0.7.67.tar.gz
```

3. Go into the directory and configure it. This is essential, as here you can enable and disable the core modules that already come with Nginx. Following is a sample configure command:

```
./configure --with-debug \
--with-http_ssl_module \
--with-http_realip_module \
--with-http_ssl_module \
--with-http_perl_module \
--with-http_stub_status_module
```

You can figure out more about what other modules and configuration flags use:

```
./configure --help
```

4. If you get an error, then you will need to install the build dependencies, depending on your system. For example, if you are running a Debian based system, you can enter the following command:

```
apt-get build-dep nginx
```

This will install all the required build dependencies, like PCRE and TLS libraries.

5. After this, you can simply go ahead and build it:

```
sudo make install
```

6. This was the plain vanilla installation! If you want to install some new modules, we take the example of the HTTP subscribe-publish module:

7. Download your module (http://pushmodule.slact.net/downloads/nginx_http_push_module-0.692.tar.gz).

8. Un-tar it at a certain location:/path/to/module.

9. Reconfigure Nginx installation:

```
./configure ..... --add-module=/path/to/module
```

The important part is to point the –add-module flag to the right module path. The rest is handled by the Nginx configuration script.

10. You can continue to build and install Nginx as shown in step 5.

```
sudo make install
```

If you have followed steps 1 to 10, it will be really easy for you to install any Nginx module.

There's more...

If you want to check that the module is installed correctly, you can enter the following command:

```
nginx -V
```

A sample output is something as shown in the following screenshot:

```
dipankar@arbitrary-main:~$ /usr/local/nginx/sbin/nginx -V
nginx version: nginx/0.7.65
built by gcc 4.4.1 (Ubuntu 4.4.1-4ubuntu9)
configure arguments: --add-module=../slact-nginx_http_push_module-90ddd57/
```

This basically gives you the compilation flags that were used to install this particular binary of Nginx, indirectly listing the various modules that were compiled into it.

Running Nginx in debug mode

Nginx is a fairly stable piece of software which has been running in production for over a decade and has built a very strong developer community around it. But, like all software there are issues and bugs which crop up under the most critical of situations. When that happens, it's usually best to reload Nginx with higher levels of error logging and if possible, in the debug mode.

How to do it...

If you want the debug mode, then you will need to compile Nginx with the debug flag (`--with-debug`). In most cases, most of the distributions have packages where Nginx is pre-compiled with debug flag. Here are the various levels of debugging that you can utilize:

```
error_log LOGFILE [debug | info | notice | warn | error | crit |
debug_core | debug_alloc | debug_mutex | debug_event | debug_http |
debug_imap];
```

Downloading the example code

You can download the example code files for all Packt books you have purchased from your account at http://www.PacktPub.com. If you purchased this book elsewhere, you can visit http://www.PacktPub.com/support and register to have the files e-mailed directly to you.

If you do not set the error log location, it will log to a compiled-in default log location. This logging is in addition to the normal error logging that you can do per site. Here is what the various specific debug flags do:

Flags	Application
debug_core	Lets you dump the core when Nginx crashes
debug_alloc	Logs all memory allocation warnings and errors
debug_mutex	Logs potential mutex issues
debug_event	Logs events module issues
debug_http	This is the default HTTP logging
debug_imap	This is the default IMAP logging

There's more...

Nginx allows us to log errors for specific IP addresses. Here is a sample configuration that will log errors from `192.168.1.1` and the IP range of `192.168.10.0/24`:

```
error_log logs/error.log;
events {
    debug_connection    192.168.1.1;
    debug_connection    192.168.10.0/24;
}
```

This is extremely useful when you want to debug in the production environment, as logging for all cases has unnecessary performance overheads. This feature allows you to not set a global debug on the `error_log`, while being able to see the debug output for specific matched IP blocks based on the user's IP address.

Easy reloading of Nginx using the CLI

Depending on the system that you have, it will offer one clean way of reloading your Nginx setup

- **Debian based**: `/etc/init.d/Nginx reload`
- **Fedora based**: `service Nginx reload`
- **FreeBSD/BSD**: `service Nginx reload`
- **Windows**: `Nginx -s reload`

All the preceding commands reload Nginx; they send a HUP signal to the main Nginx process. You can send quite a few control signals to the Nginx master process, as outlined in the following table. These let you manage some of the basic administrative tasks:

Signal	Activity
TERM,INT	Quick shutdown
QUIT	Graceful shutdown
HUP	Reload configuration, gracefully shutdown the worker processes and restart them
USR1	Reopen the log files
USR2	Upgrade the executable on the fly, when you have already installed it
WINCH	Gracefully shutdown the worker process

How to do it...

Let me run you through the simple steps of how you can reload Nginx from the command line.

1. Open a terminal on your system. Most UNIX-based systems already have fairly powerful terminals, while you can use PuTTY on Windows systems.

2. Type in `ps auxww | grep nginx`. This will output something as shown in the following screenshot:

```
dipankar@arbitrary-main:~$ ps auxww | grep nginx
root      3322  0.0  0.0  37296   596 ?        Ss   Sep23   0:00 nginx: master p
rocess /usr/local/nginx/sbin/nginx
nobody    3323  0.0  0.0  37780  1556 ?        S    Sep23   0:01 nginx: worker p
rocess
nobody    3324  0.0  0.0  37780  1444 ?        S    Sep23   0:00 nginx: worker p
rocess
dipankar  4474  0.0  0.0   3128   800 pts/2    S+   02:42   0:00 grep --color=au
to nginx
dipankar@arbitrary-main:~$
```

   If nothing comes, then it means that Nginx is not running on your system.

3. If you get the preceding output, then you can see the master process and the two worker processes (it may be more, depending on your `worker_processes` configuration). The important number is `3322`, which is basically the PID of the master process.

4. To reload Nginx, you can issue the command `kill -HUP <PID of the nginx master process>`. In this case, the PID of the master process is `3322`. This will basically read the configurations again, gracefully close your current connections, and start new worker processes. You can issue another `ps auxww | grep nginx` to see new PIDs for the worker processes (4582,4583):

```
dipankar@arbitrary-main:~$ ps auxww | grep nginx
root      3322  0.0  0.0  37440  1200 ?        Ss   Sep23   0:00 nginx: master p
rocess /usr/local/nginx/sbin/nginx
nobody    4582  0.0  0.0  37852  1140 ?        S    02:44   0:00 nginx: worker p
rocess
nobody    4583  0.0  0.0  37852  1208 ?        S    02:44   0:00 nginx: worker p
rocess
dipankar  4588  0.0  0.0   3128   796 pts/2    S+   02:44   0:00 grep --color=au
to nginx
```

5. If the worker PIDs do not change it means that you may have a problem while reloading the configuration files. Go ahead and check the Nginx error log.

This is very useful while writing scripts, which control Nginx configuration. A good example is when you are deploying code on production; you will temporarily point the site to a static landing page.

Splitting configuration files for better management

By default, when you are installing Nginx you get this one monolithic configuration file which contains a whole lot of sample configurations. Due to its extremely modular and robust designing, Nginx allows you to maintain your configuration file as a set of multiple linked files.

How to do it...

Let's take a sample configuration file `nginx.conf` and see how can it be broken into logical, maintainable pieces:

```
user         www www; #This directive determines the user and group of
the processes started
worker_processes   2;
error_log   logs/error.log;
pid         logs/nginx.pid;
events {
    worker_connections   1024;
}
http {
    include       mime.types;
    default_type  application/octet-stream;
    gzip on;
    gzip_min_length 5000;
    gzip_buffers    4 8k;
    gzip_types text/plain text/html text/css application/x-javascript
text/xml application/xml application/xml+rss text/javascript;
    gzip_proxied   any;
    gzip_comp_level 2;
    ignore_invalid_headers   on;
    server {
        listen         80;
        server_name   www.example1.com;
        location / {
            root    /var/www/www.example1.com;
            index   index.php index.html index.htm;
        }
        location ~ \.php$ {
            include conf/fcgi.conf;
            fastcgi_pass    127.0.0.1:9000;
        }
    }
}
```

The preceding configuration is basically serving a simple PHP site at
`http://www.example1.com` using FastCGI. Now we can go ahead and
split this file into the following structure:

- ▸ `nginx.conf`: The central configuration file remains
- ▸ `fcgi.conf`: This will contain all the FastCGI configurations
- ▸ `sites-enabled/`: This directory will contain all the sites that are enabled (much like Apache2's sites-enabled directory)
- ▸ `sites-available/`: This directory will contain all the sites that are not active, but available (again, much like Apache2's sites-available)
- ▸ `sites-enabled/site1.conf`: This is the sample virtual host configuration of the sample PHP site

The following code is for the new `nginx.conf`

```
user         www www;
worker_processes   2;
error_log  logs/error.log;
pid          logs/nginx.pid;
events {
        worker_connections   1024;
}
http {
        include        mime.types;
        default_type   application/octet-stream;
        gzip on;
        gzip_min_length 5000;
        gzip_buffers    4 8k;
        gzip_types text/plain text/html text/css application/x-
javascript text/xml application/xml application/xml+rss text/
javascript;
        gzip_proxied   any;
        gzip_comp_level 2;
        ignore_invalid_headers   on;
        includes sites-available/*;
}
```

If you notice, you will see how `includes` has allowed the inclusion of external configuration files. It should be noted that if we have any errors in any of the files, the Nginx server will fail to reload.

Here is the FastCGI configuration which is used by this setup; generally most Nginx installations provide a default one.

The following is the code for `fcgi.conf`:

```
fastcgi_param   QUERY_STRING         $query_string;
fastcgi_param   REQUEST_METHOD       $request_method;
fastcgi_param   CONTENT_TYPE         $content_type;
fastcgi_param   CONTENT_LENGTH       $content_length;
fastcgi_param   SCRIPT_NAME          $fastcgi_script_name;
fastcgi_param   REQUEST_URI          $request_uri;
fastcgi_param   DOCUMENT_URI         $document_uri;
fastcgi_param   DOCUMENT_ROOT        $document_root;
fastcgi_param   SERVER_PROTOCOL      $server_protocol;
fastcgi_param   GATEWAY_INTERFACE    CGI/1.1;
fastcgi_param   SERVER_SOFTWARE      nginx/$nginx_version;
fastcgi_param   REMOTE_ADDR          $remote_addr;
fastcgi_param   REMOTE_PORT          $remote_port;
fastcgi_param   SERVER_ADDR          $server_addr;
fastcgi_param   SERVER_PORT          $server_port;
fastcgi_param   SERVER_NAME          $server_name;
fastcgi_index   index.php ;
fastcgi_param   SCRIPT_FILENAME   $document_root$fastcgi_script_name ;

# PHP only, required if PHP was built with --enable-force-cgi-redirect
fastcgi_param   REDIRECT_STATUS      200;
fastcgi_connect_timeout 60;
fastcgi_send_timeout 180;
fastcgi_read_timeout 180;
fastcgi_buffer_size 128k;
fastcgi_buffers 4 256k;
fastcgi_busy_buffers_size 256k;
fastcgi_temp_file_write_size 256k;
fastcgi_intercept_errors on;
```

The following is the code for `sites-enabled/site1.conf`:

```
server {
    listen        80;
    server_name   www.example1.com;
    location / {
        root    /var/www/www.example1.com;
        index   index.php index.html index.htm;
    }
    location ~ \.php$ {
        include conf/fcgi.conf;
        fastcgi_pass    127.0.0.1:9000;
    }
}
```

This sort of a file arrangement allows clean separation of the main configuration and the auxiliary ones. It also promotes structured thinking, which is useful when you have to quickly switch or deploy sites.

We will go over the various configurations that you see in these files in other chapters. For example, `fcgi.conf` is covered in the recipe to get PHP working with Nginx using FastCGI.

Setting up multiple virtual hosts

Usually any web server hosts one or more domains, and Nginx, like any good web server, allows you to easily configure as many virtual hosts as you want.

How to do it...

Let's take a simple example. You want to set up a simple set of webpages on `www.example1.com`. Here is the sample configuration which needs to go into the `sites-enabled/site1.conf`:

```
server {
    listen 80;
    server_name www.example1.com example1.com;
    access_log /var/log/Nginx/example1.com/access.log;
    error_log /var/log/Nginx/example1.com/error.log;
    location / {
            root /var/www/www.example1.com;
            index index.html index.htm;
    }
}
```

How it works...

So let's see how this works. The `listen` defines the port on which the web server is listening (in this case, its 80)! The `server_name` lets you easily define the domain that maps to this virtual host configuration. Inside, you can start defining how the virtual host works. In this case it serves set of HTML pages from the `/var/www/www.example1.com` directory.

So when you reload your Nginx configuration assuming that your DNS records point correctly at your server, you should see your HTML pages load when you access the web address (in this case, `http://www.example1.com`).

There's more...

Here is a quick checklist to get you started:

1. Create a simple directory with the HTML files.
2. Create a simple configuration file containing the virtual host configuration for `www.example1.com`.
3. Reload Nginx.
4. Point your DNS server to the correct server running Nginx.
5. Load `www.example1.com`.

Setting up a default catch-all virtual host

Once you are comfortable setting up the virtual hosts, you will end up in a situation where you have a lot of domains pointing at the IP. In addition to the domains, you would also have the web server responding to the IP addresses it hosts, and many other unused subdomains of the domains pointing at it. We can take a look at this with a simple example, so you have `http://www.example1.com` pointing at the IP address, you have configured a virtual host to handle the domains `www.example1.com` and `example1.com`. In such a scenario, when the user types in `abc.example1.com` or an IP address the web server will not be able to serve the relevant content (be it 404 or some other promotional page).

How to do it...

For situations like the one above, one can utilize the default catchall virtual host that Nginx provides; here is a simple example where this default catchall virtual host serves a simple set of web pages.

The following is the code for `sites-enabled/default.conf`:

```
server {
    listen   80 default;
    server_name   _;
    location / {
            root /var/www/default;
            index index.html index.htm;
    }
}
```

How it works...

The key thing to note is the fact that you are listening on the default port and that the `server_name` is "_" which is the catchall mechanism. So whenever the user enters a domain for which you have no defined virtual host, pages will get server from the `/var/www/default` directory.

Using wildcards in virtual hosts

Imagine a situation where you need to create an application that needs to serve dynamic pages on subdomains! In that case, you will need to set up a virtual host in Nginx that can utilize wildcards. Nginx has been made ground up to handle such a scenario. So let's take our favorite example of `http://www.example1.com`. Let's say you are building an application that needs to handle the various subdomains such as `a.example1.com`, `b.example1.com`, and so on. The following configuration would let the application behind handle all these various subdomains.

How to do it...

You will need to set a wildcard on the DNS entry. Without the DNS entries, the domain (and subdomains) will never resolve to your server IP. A sample DNS entry is given below which points the domain `http://example1.com` to the IP `69.9.64.11`:

```
example1.com.  IN A 69.9.64.11
```

Once you know how your DNS works, you can add this to your `nginx.conf` inside the http section:

```
server {
    listen 80;
    server_name example1.com *.example1.com;
    location / {
            . . . . . . . .
    }
}
```

How it works...

The important part to note is that in this case, you are serving all the subdomains using the same code base. We have also set the virtual host to serve the non-www domain as well (`example1.com` which is different from `www.example1.com`).

So when you type `a.example1.com`, your web application will receive `a.example1.com` as the domain that was requested from the web server and it can process the HTTP response accordingly.

Setting up the number of worker processes correctly

Nginx like any other UNIX-based server software, works by spawning multiple processes and allows the configuration of various parameters around them as well. One of the basic configurations is the number of worker processes spawned! It is by far one of the first things that one has to configure in Nginx.

How to do it...

This particular configuration can be found at the top of the sample configuration file `nginx.conf`:

```
user        www www;
worker_processes  5;
error_log  logs/error.log;
pid         logs/nginx.pid;
worker_rlimit_nofile 8192;
events {
  worker_connections  4096;
}
```

In the preceding configuration, we can see how the various process configurations work. You first set the UNIX user under which the process runs, then you can set the number of worker processes that Nginx needs to spawn, after that we have some file locations where the errors are logged and the PIDs (process IDs) are saved.

How it works...

By default, `worker_processes` is set at 2. It is a crucial setting in a high performance environment as Nginx uses it for the following reasons:

- It uses SMP, which allows you to efficiently use multi-cores or multi-processors systems very efficiently and have a definite performance gain.

- It increases the number of processes decreases latency as workers get blocked on disk I/O.

- It limits the number of connections per process when any of the various supported event types are used. A worker process cannot have more connections than specified by the `worker_connections` directive.

There's more...

It is recommended that you set `worker_processes` as the number of cores available on your server. If you know the values of `worker_processes` and `worker_connections`, one can easily calculate the maximum number of connections that Nginx can handle in the current setup.

Maximum clients = `worker_processes` * `worker_connections`

Increasing the size of uploaded files

Usually when you are running a site where the user uploads a lot of files, you will see that when they upload a file which is more than 1MB in size you get an Nginx error stating, "Request entity too Large" (413), as shown in the following screenshot. We will look at how Nginx can be configured to handle larger uploads.

How to do it...

This is controlled by one simple part of the Nginx configuration. You can simply paste this in the server part of the Nginx configuration:

```
client_max_body_size 100M; # M stands for megabytes
```

This preceding configuration will allow you to upload a 100 megabyte file. Anything more than that, and you will receive a 413. You can set this to any value which is less than the available disk space to Nginx, which is primarily because Nginx downloads the file to a temporary location before forwarding it to the backend application.

There's more...

Nginx also lets us control other factors related to people uploading files on the web application, like timeouts in case the client has a slow connection. A slow client can keep one of your application threads busy and thus potentially slow down your application. This is a problem that is experienced on all the heavy multimedia user-driven sites, where the consumer uploads all kinds of rich data such as images, documents, videos, and so on. So it is sensible to set low timeouts.

```
client_body_timeout 60; # parameter in seconds
client_body_buffer_size 8k;
client_header_timeout 60; # parameter in seconds
client_header_buffer_size 1k;
```

So, here the first two settings help you control the timeout when the body is not received at one read-step (basically, if the server is queried and no response comes back). Similarly, you can set the timeout for the HTTP header as well. The following table lists out the various directives and limits you can set around client uploading.

Directive	Use
client_body_in_file_only	This directive forces Nginx to always store a client request body in temporary disk files, even if the file size is 0. The file will not be removed at request completion.
client_body_in_single_ buffer	This directive specifies whether to keep the whole body in a single client request buffer.
client_body_buffer_size	This directive specifies the client request body buffer size. If the request body is more than the buffer, then the entire request body or some part is written in a temporary file.
client_body_temp_path	This directive assigns the directory for storing the temporary files in it with the body of the request.
client_body_timeout	This directive sets the read timeout for the request body from client.
client_header_buffer_size	This directive sets the header buffer size for the request header from client.
client_header_timeout	This directive assigns timeout with reading of the title of the request of client.
client_max_body_size	This directive assigns the maximum accepted body size of client request, indicated by the line Content-Length in the header of request.

Using dynamic SSI for simple sites

With the advent of modern feature-full web servers, most of them have Server-Side Includes (SSI) built in. Nginx provides easy SSI support which can let you do pretty much all basic web stuff.

How to do it...

Let's take a simple example and start understanding what one can achieve with it.

1. Add the following code to the `nginx.conf` file:

```
server {
        ..…
        location / {
                ssi on;
                root /var/www/www.example1.com;
        }
}
```

2. Add the following code to the `index.html` file:

```
<html>
<body>
  <!--# block name="header_default" -->
  the header testing
 <!--# endblock -->
 <!--# include file="header.html" stub="header_default" →
<!--# echo var="name" default="no" -->
 <!--# include file="footer.html"-->
</body>
</html>
```

3. Add the following code to the `header.html` file:

```
<h2>Simple header</h2>
```

4. Add the following code to the `footer.html` file:

```
<h2>Simple footer</h2>
```

How it works...

This is a simple example where we can see that you can simply include some partials in the larger page, and in addition to that you can create block as well within the page. So the `<block>` directive allows you to create silent blocks that can be included later, while the `<include>` directive can be used to include HTML partials from other files, or even URL end points. The `<echo>` directive is used to output certain variables from within the Nginx context.

There's more...

You can utilize this feature for all kinds of interesting setups where:

- You are serving different blocks of HTML for different browsers types
- You want to optimize and speed up certain common blocks of the sites
- You want to build a simple site with template inheritance without installing any other scripting language

Adding content before and after a particular page

Today, in most of the sites that we visit, the webpage structure is formally divided into a set of boxes. Usually, all sites have a static header and a footer block. Here, in this following page you can see the YUI builder generating the basic framework of such a page.

In such a scenario, Nginx has a really useful way of adding content before and after it serves a certain page. This will potentially allow you to separate the various blocks and optimize their performance individually, as well.

Let's have a look at an example page:

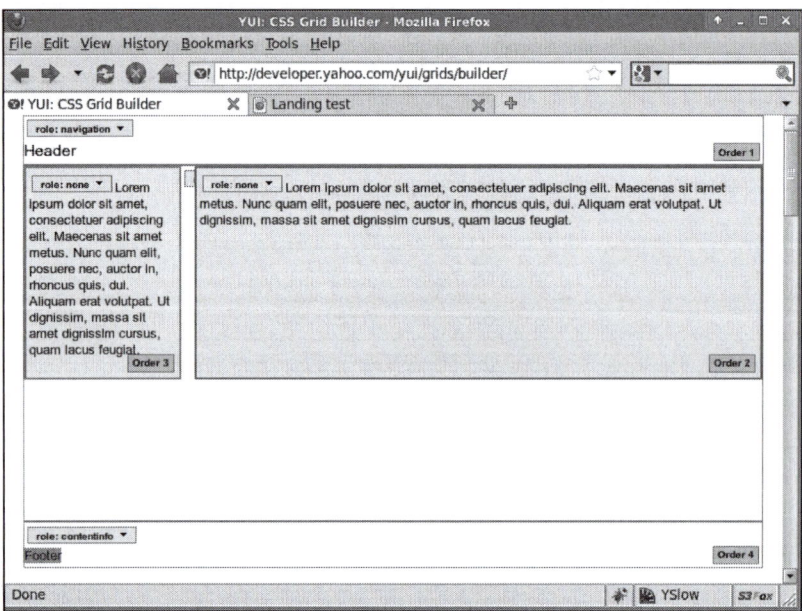

So here we want to insert the header block before the content, and then append the footer block:

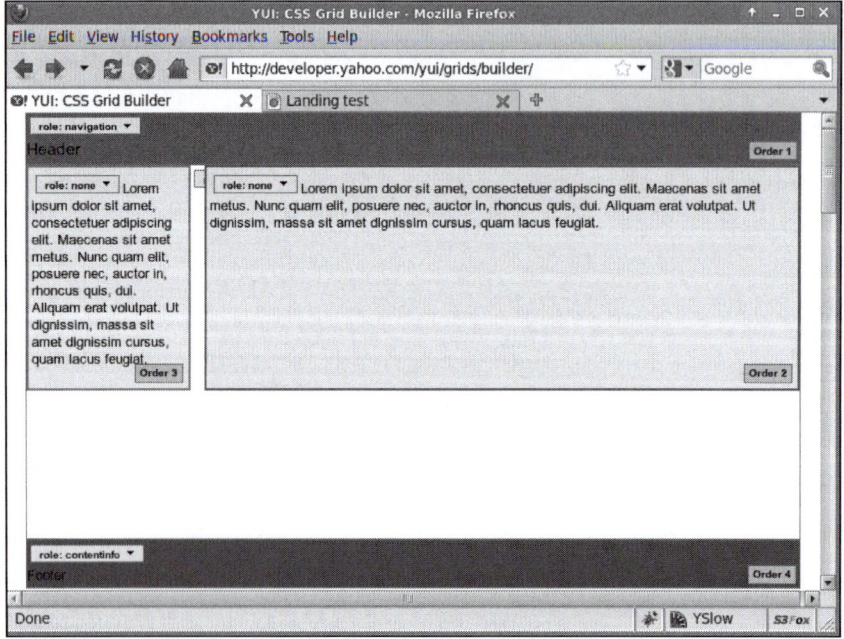

How to do it...

The sample configuration for this particular page would look like this:

```
server {
    listen 80;
    server_name www.example1.com;
    location / {
            add_before_body    /red_block
            add_after_body     /blue_block;
            ...
    }
    location /red_block/ {
            ...
    }
    location /blue_block/ {
            ....
    }
}
```

This can act as a performance enhancer by allowing you to load CSS based upon the browser only. There can be cases where you want to introduce something into the header or the footer on short notice, without modifying your backend application. This provides an easy fix for those situations.

This module is not installed by default and it is necessary to enable it when building Nginx.
```
./configure –with-http_addition_module
```

Enabling auto indexing of a directory

Nginx has an inbuilt auto-indexing module. Any request where the index file is not found will route to this module. This is similar to the directory listing that Apache displays.

How to do it...

Here is the example of one such Nginx directory listing. It is pretty useful when you want to share some files over your local network. To start auto index on any directory all you need to do is to carry out the following example and place it in the server section of the Nginx configuration file:

```
server {
    location 80;
```

```
server_name www.example1.com;
location / {
        root /var/www/test;
        autoindex on;
}
}
```

How it works...

This will simply enable auto indexing when the user types in `http://www.example1.com`. You can also control some other things in the listings in this way:

```
autoindex_exact_size off;
```

This will turn off the exact file size listing and will only show the estimated sizes. This can be useful when you are worried about file privacy issues.

```
autoindex_localtime on;
```

This will represent the timestamps on the files as your local server time (it is GMT by default):

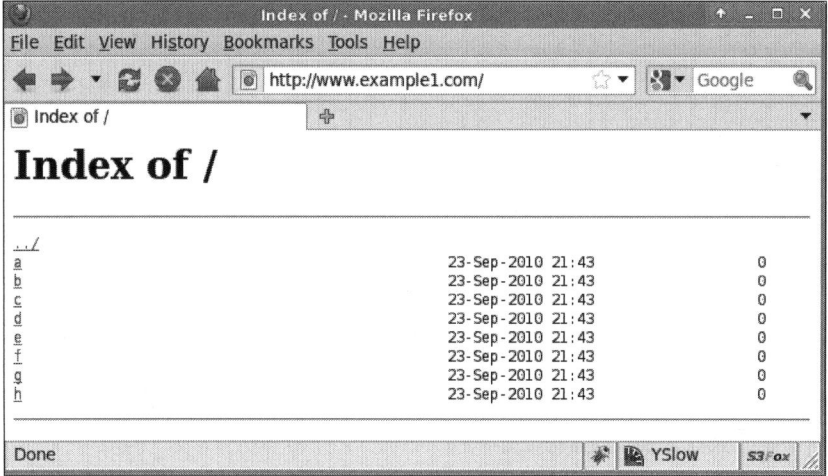

This image displays a sample index auto-generated by Nginx using the preceding configuration. You can see the filenames, timestamp, and the file sizes as the three data columns.

Serving any random web page from a directory

There has been a recent trend for a lot of sites to test out their new pages based upon the A/B methodology. You can explore more about its history and the various companies that have adopted this successfully as a part of their development process at `http://en.wikipedia.org/wiki/A/B_testing`. In this practice, you have a set of pages and some metric (such as number of registrations, or the number of clicks on a particular element). Then you go about getting people to randomly visit these pages and get data about their behavior on them. This lets you iteratively improve the page and the elements on them.

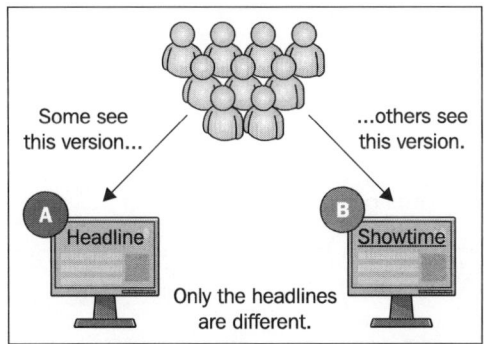

Nginx has something that will let you to run your own A-B test without writing any code at all. It allows you to randomly select any web page from a directory and display it.

How to do it...

Let's have a look at a sample configuration which needs to be placed within the HTTP section of the Nginx configuration:

```
server {
    listen 80;
    server_name www.example1.com;
    location  /  {
            root /var/www/www.example1.com/test_index;
            random_index   on;
    }
}
```

How it works...

Let's assume that you have some files in the `/var/www/www.example1.com/test_index` directory. When you turn on the random index it will scan the directory and then send a randomly picked file instead of the default `index.html`. The only exceptions are plain files. Whole filenames which start with a dot will not be part of the site of files to be picked from.

So here are two sample test pages, with slightly differing headers. Notice that the URLs are the same. So it will let you determine if the end user is clicking through more with the red link or the blue link using pure statistical methods:

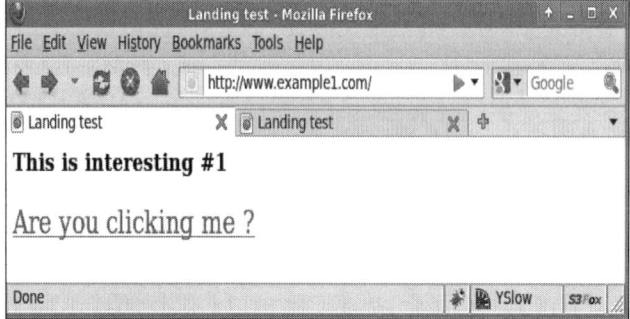

The preceding screenshot displays `A.html` on opening the site. There is equal probability of opening both the pages, much like the tossing of a coin and getting heads or tails.

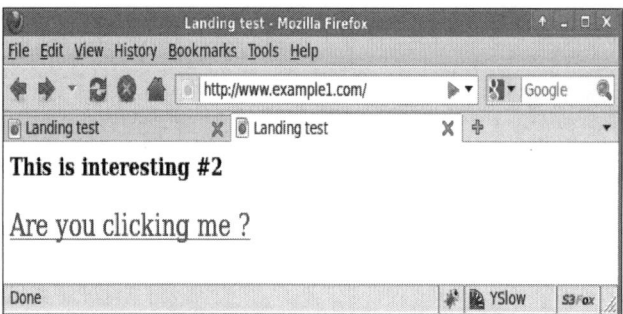

So, using the A-B testing as an example, you can set an `A.html` and a `B.html`, which would be served to the user randomly. It would allow you to easily measure a lot of interesting client behavior by simply analyzing the Nginx access logs.

Serving cookies for identifying and logging users

Nginx has a useful functionality of serving cookies for identifying users. This is very useful in tracking anonymous user behavior in case a website does not want to employ external analytics software. This module is compatible with the `mod_uid` module in Apache2, which provides a similar functionality.

How to do it...

Here is a sample configuration for this module. This goes in the server section of the configuration:

```
userid          on;
userid_name     uid;
userid_domain   example1.com;
userid_path     /;
userid_expires  365d;
userid_p3p      'policyref="/w3c/p3p.xml", CP="CUR ADM OUR NOR STA
NID"';
```

How it works...

Now let's see and understand what the various directives are about. The first `userid` directive enables this module; the second assigns a name to the cookie which is going to be written on the client side. The next three directives are the standard cookie information that is needed (the primary domain, the path, and the time of expiry). The last directive enables the browser to understand the privacy practices that the website follows. This is done by using the P3P protocol which allows websites to declare their intended usage that they collect about the user. It is basically an XML file that allows you to programmatically display your privacy policy. The following code is a simple example configuration of how you can define a policy where the data is removed after 4 months:

```
<META xmlns="http://www.w3.org/2002/01/P3Pv1">
  <POLICY-REFERENCES>
    <EXPIRY max-age="10000000"/><!-- about four months -->
  </POLICY-REFERENCES>
</META>
```

This XML put on the server will objectively define the privacy policies of the site to the incoming bots or users.

There's more...

On enabling this module, some variables are available in the Nginx configuration which allow you do fairly interesting things. You have access to some variables in the configuration contest, like $uid_got, $uid_set.

These can be used for writing interesting rewrite rules. A simple application using these variables is to log the users coming on your site and then determining the user bounce rates on your website by parsing the logs.

Re-encoding the response to another encoding

File encoding is a major issue on most websites, a lot of time the database (MySQL in most cases) is configured to run using the Latin-1 encoding instead of the UTF-8 encoding that is the prevalent standard. Nginx provides an easy solution for changing your web page encoding on-the-fly, so that your users do not end up with garbled characters on your website

How to do it...

All you need to do is to place this in the server section of your Nginx configuration:

```
charset          windows-1251;
source_charset  koi8-r;
```

How it works...

This basically defines the fact that the source character set is koi8-r. If the encoding is different from the charset character set, then re-encoding is carried out. In case your original response already has a "Content-Type" header present then you will need to use the following to override and do the re-encoding:

```
overrride_charset on;
```

There's more...

You can also decide how the re-encoding happens by defining a character mapping. A simple example is the following:

```
charset_map  koi8-r  windows-1251 {
   C0   FE ; # small yu
   C1   E0 ; # small a
   C2   E1 ; # small b
```

```
    C3   F6 ; # small ts
    # ...
}
```

Nginx lets you do these neat little things that can make your site more accessible and usable for the end-user.

Enabling Gzip compression on some content types

As the Web has evolved, we have had improvements in web server and browser technologies. In recent times, with the booming consumer Internet market, the web application has had to become faster.

Compression techniques, which were already present, have come of age and now most sites enable a fairly high degree of compression on the pages they serve. Nginx being state of the art, has Gzip compression and allows a whole lot of options on how to go about it.

How to do it...

You will need to modify your Nginx configuration file and add the following directives:

```
http {
    gzip               on;
    gzip_min_length    1000;
    gzip_comp_level 6;
    gzip_proxied       expired no-cache no-store private auth;
    gzip_types         text/plain application/xml;
    gzip_disable       "MSIE [1-6]\.";
    server {
        ....
    }
}
```

How it works...

This sample configuration allows you to turn on the Gzip compression of the outgoing page for all pages which are over 1000 bytes. This limit is set because compression technology performance degrades as the page size becomes smaller. You can then set the various MIME types for which the compression should occur; this particular example will compress only plain text files and XML files.

Older browsers are not the best when it comes to utilizing this, and you can disable Gzip depending on the browser type. One of the most interesting settings is the level of compression where you need to make a choice between the amount of CPU that you want to spend on compressing and serving the pages (*the higher this number, more of your CPU time will go towards compressing and sending pages*). It is recommended to follow a middle path on this particular setting; the client also spends more CPU time decompressing the page if you set this. A sensible setting of this value would be six.

There's more...

For proxy requests, `gzip_proxied` actually allows or disallows the compression of the response of the proxy request based on the request and the response. You can use the following parameters:

parameter	Function
off	Disables compression for all proxy requests
expired	Enables compression, if the `Expires` header prevents caching
no-cache	Enables compression if `Cache-Control` header contains `no-cache`
no-store	Enables compression if `Cache-Control` header contains `no-store`
private	Enables compression if `Cache-Control` header contains `private`
no_last_modified	Enables compression if `Last-Modified` isn't set
no_etag	Enables compression if there is no `ETag` header
auth	Enables compression if there is an `Authorization` header
any	Enables compression for all requests

So in the preceding example (`expired no-cache no-store private auth`) it is clear that the compression is enabled when the `Expires` header prevents caching, when the `Cache-Control` contains `no-cache`, `no-store`, or `private`, and when there is an `Authorization` header present. This allows tremendous control on how the compression is delivered to the client's browser.

Setting up 404 and other error pages

All web applications have errors and missing pages, and Nginx has easy methods of ensuring that the end user has a good experience when the application does not respond correctly. It successfully handles all the HTTP errors with default pages, which can gracefully notify the users that something has gone wrong.

How to do it...

Nginx allows you to do pretty interesting things with error pages. Following are some example configurations which can be placed within the HTTP or server section.

We are also going to define a named location using the "@" prefix after location. These locations are not used during the normal processing of any request and are intended to only process internally redirected requests.

```
location @fallback (
    proxy_pass http://backend;
)
error_page    404            /404.html;
error_page    502 503 504   /50x.html;
error_page    403            http://example1.com/forbidden.html;
error_page    404            = @fallback;
error_page 404 =200 /.empty.gif;
```

How it works...

The first example allows you to map a simple 404 page to a simple HTML. The next example allows the mapping of various application error codes to another generic application error HTML page. You can also map the error page to some other external site all together (`http://example1.com/forbidden.html`). The fourth example allows you to map the page to another location, defined as `@fallback`. The last example is interesting as it actually allows you to change the response code to a 200 (HTTP OK). This is useful in situations where you have excessive 404 pages on the site, and would prefer not sending a 404 back as reply, but a 200 with a very small GIF file in return.

You can utilize this very effectively to give the end user a better experience when they inadvertently reach dead ends and application errors on your site.

If you do not set these error pages correctly, you will get the default Nginx error pages which may not be useful to the user and may turn them away.

2
All About Rewrites: The Rewrite Module

In this chapter, we will cover:

- ▶ Setting up a simple redirect
- ▶ Using variables in your rewrite
- ▶ Using cookies for your rewrites
- ▶ Using browser agents for your rewrites
- ▶ Using rate limits as a condition for rewrites
- ▶ Blocking requests based on HTTP referrers
- ▶ Serving maintenance page when deploying
- ▶ Setting up a WordPress site with static file serving
- ▶ Setting up a Drupal site with static file serving
- ▶ Setting up a Magento site with static file serving
- ▶ Converting your apache .htaccess into Nginx rewrites
- ▶ Using maps to make configurations cleaner

Introduction

This chapter is devoted to the rewrite module; it will teach you the basics and also allow you to configure various commonly available web development frameworks to work correctly with your Nginx setup using the correct rewrite rules.

Setting up a simple redirect

A lot of sites undergo changes, and in some cases complete rewriting. In most cases the earlier contents URLs would have changed, leading to loss of SEO and, of course, inconvenience for older clients. This recipe will help you write simple rewrites so that you can ensure that your new site has all the redirect working.

How to do it...

Let's take a simple example of a site called `http://www.example1.com`. It earlier had a page called `http://www.example1.com/blog/test-post.html` and now it's been redone. The new blog has a different URL scheme and this old post is at the following location: `http://www.example1.com/blog/test-post/`. It may look like a simple change, but when an older bookmarked user visits the older URL they would get a 404 error page. The configuration change below will easily let you rewrite the older URL to the new one:

```
server {
    server_name www.example1.com;
    ...
    rewrite  ^/blog/test-post.html$  /blog/test-post/  permanent;
    location ~ .php$ {
        ...
    }
}
```

How it works...

This creates a permanent redirection [301] rule for the older URL and makes it point to the new one. Over time this can be removed as permanent redirects changes the bookmarks and makes sure that people/crawlers do not keep coming back to the older URL.

There's more...

You can also do a temporary redirection which is the 302 redirection by removing the permanent keyword that is:

```
rewrite  ^/blog/test-post.html$  /blog/test-post/ ;
```

This means that the browser will not update the bookmark and also the search crawlers will not update the new URL as the primary one for the content on the page.

Using variables in your rewrite

Now that we are comfortable with the basics, we can go ahead and write more interesting rewrites using conditions based on various variables accessible inside the configuration. We will look at a simple example where we check for the presence of a particular GET parameter in the URI, in the presence of which we rewrite to a special URL.

How to do it...

We will use the following piece of configuration to create the conditional rewrite:

```
location / {
    ...
    If ($arg_special ~* (beta|alpha|gamma) ) {
        rewrite ^(.*)$ http://www.example1.com/greek/$1/;
    }
}
```

How it works...

If you type in any URL which has a GET parameter special (for example, `http://www.example.com/?special=beta&test=test1`) it will show a corresponding special page for beta. This is very useful if you want to hide certain parts of your site or make it accessible only by using a basic key in the parameter.

There's more...

As seen above, you can configure a lot more variables available to you in the HTTP header. Here is a list of more variables that we can access to write more interesting rules.

Variable	Description
`$arg_PARAMETER`	This variable contains the value of the GET request variable PARAMETER if present in the query string.
`$args`	This variable contains the query string in the URL, for example `foo=123&bar=blahblah` if the URL is `http://example1.com/? foo=123&bar=blahblah`
`$binary_remote_addr`	The address of the client in binary form.
`$body_bytes_sent`	The bytes of the body sent.
`$content_length`	This variable is equal to line Content-Length in the header of request.
`$content_type`	This variable is equal to line Content-Type in the header of request.

Variable	Description
`$document_root`	This variable is equal to the value of directive root for the current request.
`$document_uri`	The same as `$uri`.
`$host`	This variable contains the value of the `'Host'` value in the request header, or the name of the server processing if the `'Host'` value is not available.
`$http_HEADER`	The value of the HTTP header HEADER when converted to lowercase and with "dashes" converted to "underscores", for example, `$http_user_agent`, `$http_referer`.
`$is_args`	Evaluates to "?" if `$args` is set, returns "" otherwise.
`$request_uri`	This variable is equal to the *original* request URI as received from the client including the args. It cannot be modified. Look at `$uri` for the post-rewrite/altered URI. Does not include host name. Example: "`/foo/bar.php?arg=baz`".

`$scheme`	The HTTP scheme (that is http, https). Evaluated only on demand, for example:
	`rewrite ^(.+)$ $scheme://example.com$1`
	`redirect;`

`$server_addr`	This variable contains the server address. It is advisable to indicate addresses correctly in the listen directive and use the bind parameter so that a system call is not made every time this variable is accessed.
`$server_name`	The name of the server.
`$server_port`	This variable is equal to the port of the server, to which the request arrived.
`$server_protocol`	This variable is equal to the protocol of request, usually this is HTTP/1.0 or HTTP/1.1.
`$uri`	This variable is equal to current URI in the request (without arguments, those are in `$args`.) It can differ from `$request_uri` which is what is sent by the browser. Examples of how it can be modified are internal redirects, or with the use of index. Does not include host name. Example: "`/foo/bar.html`"

Using cookies for your rewrites

Most websites today use their cookies to effectively track and interact with the client's browser. Nginx with its powerful rewrite module, allows us to write some interesting rules with the information that may exist in the browser cookies. You can check out the various cookies on your browser through the preferences.

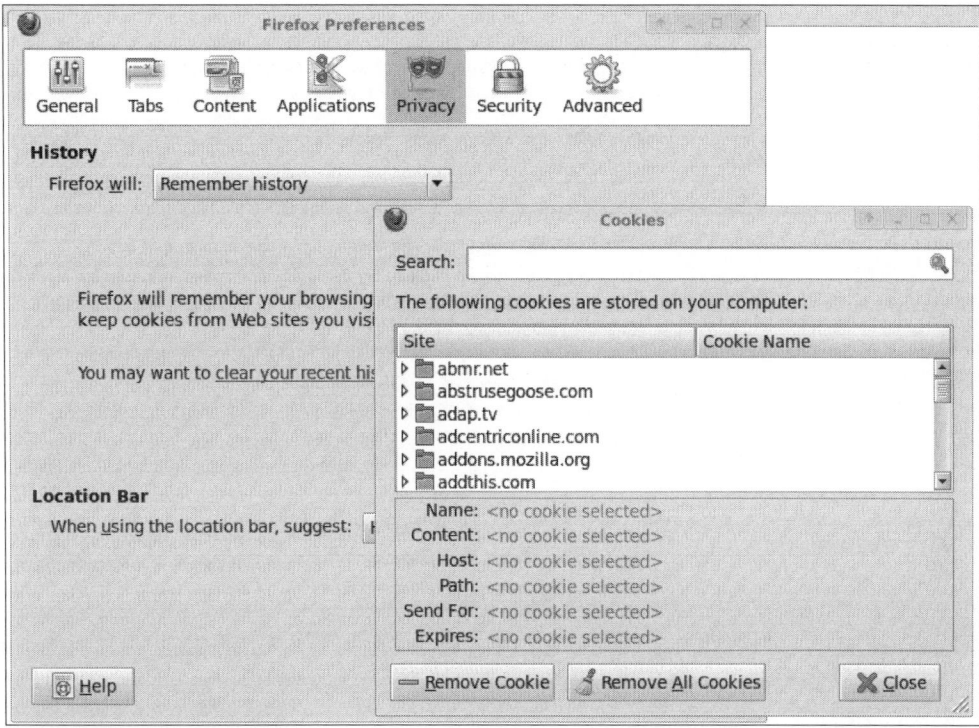

How to do it...

We can take the simple example of a site which is running the staging and production versions on the same Nginx instance. Based upon the cookie, the URL is rewritten into the correct one. The following snippet will allow you to switch sites based upon what is in the cookie:

```
if ($cookie_env ~* "testing") {
        rewrite ^(.*)$   /testing/$1;
}
 if ($cookie_env ~* "staging") {
        rewrite ^(.*)$   /staging/$1;
}
if ($cookie_env ~* "production") {
        rewrite ^(.*)$   /production/$1;
}
```

How it works...

In the above configuration the cookie value is checked for the type of setup that the user is accessing. This cookie is set on the user logging in by the application, so a testing user will be able to access cutting-edge features, while a staging user will be able to access beta features for testing only, and the normal users will continue to use the stable production system.

Using browser agents for your rewrites

In this recipe we will see how we can utilize rewrites for displaying alternative sites based on the user agent of the client's browser. We can take the example of a very flashy site that wants to display different sets of pages based upon the browser that the client is using. The following two screenshots display how `facebook.com` appears on a normal desktop browser and on an iPhone; the URL however remains the same.

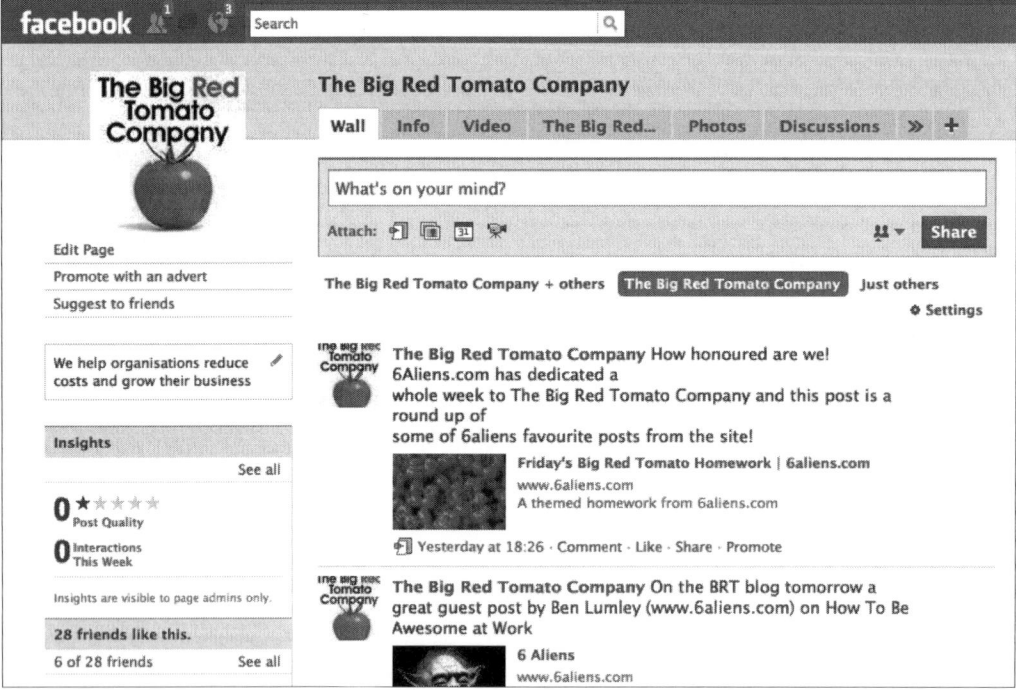

In the preceding screenshot, we are looking at the full browser version of Facebook, and you can see a fairly wide-screen site. In the following screenshot, we can see the mobile version of Facebook which clearly lets go of a lot of functionality because of the reduced screen-size.

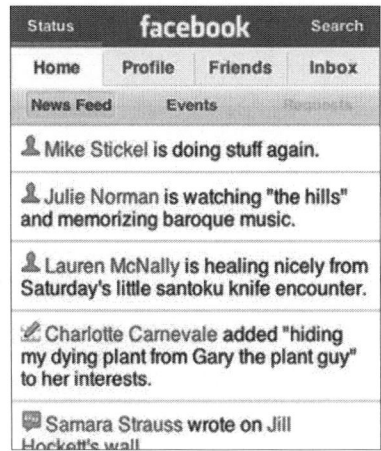

How to do it...

The simple example that we take is of an iPhone surfing the website and how you can actually rewrite the URL to show them a completely iPhone-compatible website. The configuration below is a great start for it!

```
location / {
  ...
if ($http_user_agent ~* '(iPhone|iPod)') {
    set $iphone_request '1';
}
if ($iphone_request = '1') {
    rewrite ^.+ http://m.example1.com/$uri;
}
}
```

How it works...

The idea is simple. What it allows is checking the HTTP USER AGENT header that already comes to us. We see if it is an iPhone or an iPod browser. If that is the case, we actually set a variable to some value. If that variable is "1", we go ahead and rewrite the URL to the mobile version of the site.

Using rate limits as a condition for rewrites

Nginx has some really interesting built-in features around rate limiting requests. This recipe will help you understand how exactly you can control the requests to your application, thereby maintaining a certain quality of service to your users even under significant loads.

Nginx lets you define zones that act as storage area for the state of sessions. The value of the session key is decided by the chosen variable which, is usually the IP or the hostname of the client.

How to do it...

In this example, we will see how we can rate limit based on certain parameters, like the user agent.

```
location / {
. . .
if ($http_user_agent ~ "MSIE") {
                limit_rate 5k;
}
}
```

How it works...

In the preceding example we check if the user agent contains MSIE, in which case it will rate limit the transfer to 5000 bytes only.

There's more...

You can also set up request based rate limiting by using the following snippet:

```
http {
    limit_req_zone  $binary_remote_addr  zone=one:10m  rate=1r/s;
    ...
    server {
        ...
        location / {
            limit_req  zone=one  burst=5;
        }
}
```

The above configuration creates a zone called one, which has a session storage size of 10MB allocated to it and allows a rate of one request per second in this particular configuration. In case any request comes that is outside of the rate limit that cannot be served, it will get a "Service unavailable" 503 page. You can store approximately 16000 sessions in a 1MB zone. You can choose to create as many zones as you require for your system.

Blocking requests based on HTTP referrers

In this recipe, we will take the example of writing a rule which will look at your HTTP REFERER header line of the request and block spammers on your site.

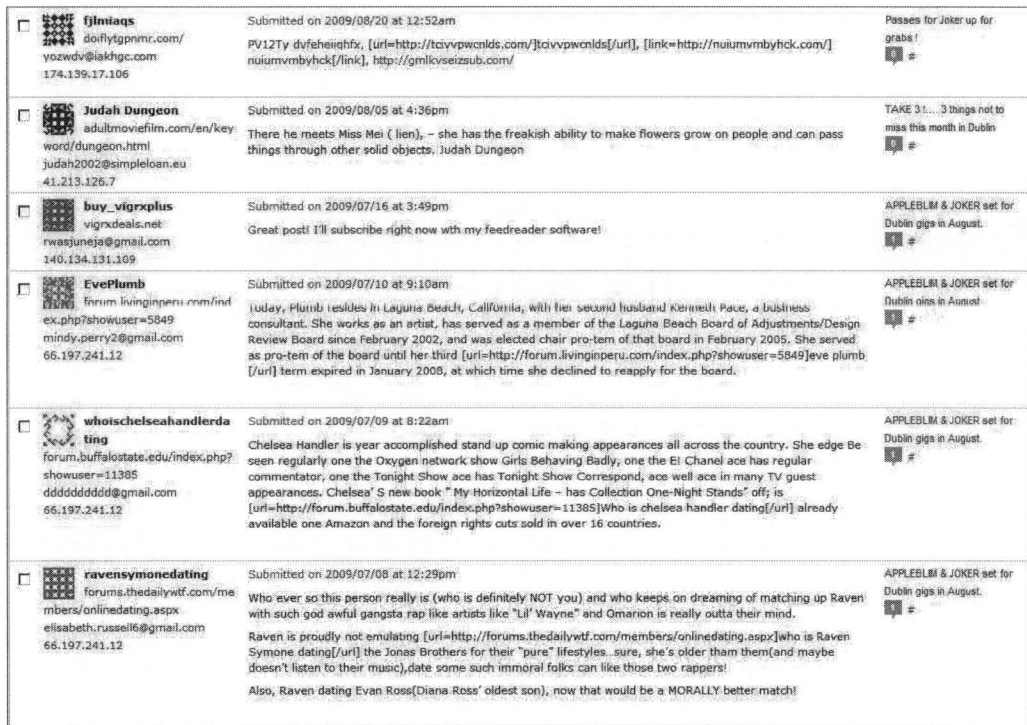

The preceding screenshot displays the spam comments on a blog for a single day; these have been made by automated bots which are trying to get linkbacks for their various properties. These techniques fall under the dark aspects of SEO.

How to do it...

To block spammer bots from visiting your site, you can use the following code snippet inside the location part of your configuration:

```
location / {
    ...
    if ($http_referer ~* (babes|click|diamond|forsale|girl|jewelry|lo
ve|nudit|organic|poker|porn|poweroversoftware|sex|teen|video|webcam|z
ippo)) {
return 403;
}
}
```

How it works...

This basically has a look at the $http_referer variable and matches it with the various keywords provided. This is a very effective in ensuring that you do not have a lot of spam in your system linking back to bad sites! In case the keywords do match, it returns a 403 client error.

Serving maintenance page when deploying

One of the few things that most sites need to do is deploy code, and usually do it when the site is running on production. Nginx is really amazing in terms of how it can easily reload its configuration without terminating the client connections. You can have a look at the reloading recipe in the previous chapter to know more. In this recipe, we will have a look at a simple way of setting up a system which can make your deployment pain free for the end user and you as well!

How to do it...

Let's run through step-by-step what one needs to do to make a working deployment. In the process the various configuration changes will also be outlined.

1. Create a directory which has the temporary "Coming back soon" HTML file. Let's call this `/var/www/www.example1.com/deployment/` and the file is `index.html`.

2. You need to create an alternative configuration file which will be called `temporary.conf`. This file basically replaces the server configuration for `www.example1.com` with the following:

```
server {
    server_name www.example1.com;
    location / {
        index index.html;
        root /var/www/www.example1.com/deployment/;
        rewrite ^(.*)$ http://www.example1.com/;
    }
}
```

3. Now we can write a small script for deployment. It will basically put the site into a temporary mode and then update your codebase. After the code update, it will simply copy the older production configuration and reload Nginx.

```
!#/bin/bash
mv /etc/nginx/nginx.conf /etc/nginx/nginx_temp.conf
mv /etc/nginx/temporary.conf /etc/nginx/nginx.conf
kill -HUP `cat /var/log/nqinx/nqinx.pid`
#<deploy the code>
# Restart the Fcgi / WSGI backend
mv /etc/nginx/nginx_temp.conf /etc/nginx/nginx.conf
kill -HUP `cat /var/log/nginx/nginx.pid`
```

How it works...

In this recipe, we simply use our earlier learned techniques and combine them with some nifty bash scripting to write a simple deployment script. The idea is to rewrite all the URLs to the maintenance page when the site is being deployed, and once done with the backend code deployment we revert back to the older production configuration.

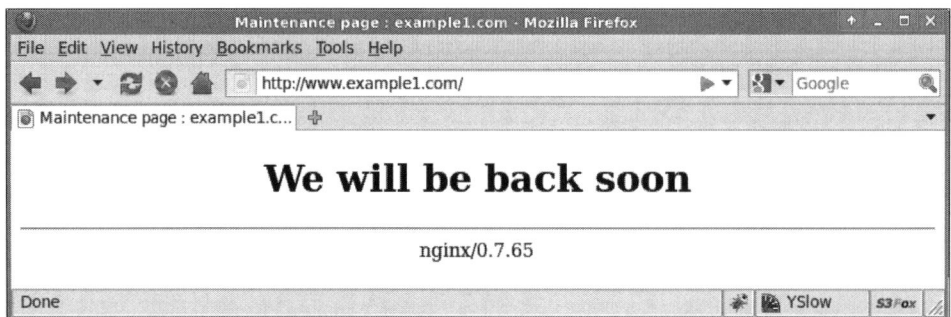

Setting up a WordPress site with static file serving

WordPress is one of the world's leading blogging systems, and is pretty much the defacto standard today. It has a fairly easy setup with Apache2 and makes setting up of clean URLs pretty simple as well. However, with Nginx, (and PHP over fcgi) setting up WordPress with clean URLs requires some amount of work. My own blog is running on WordPress with Nginx!

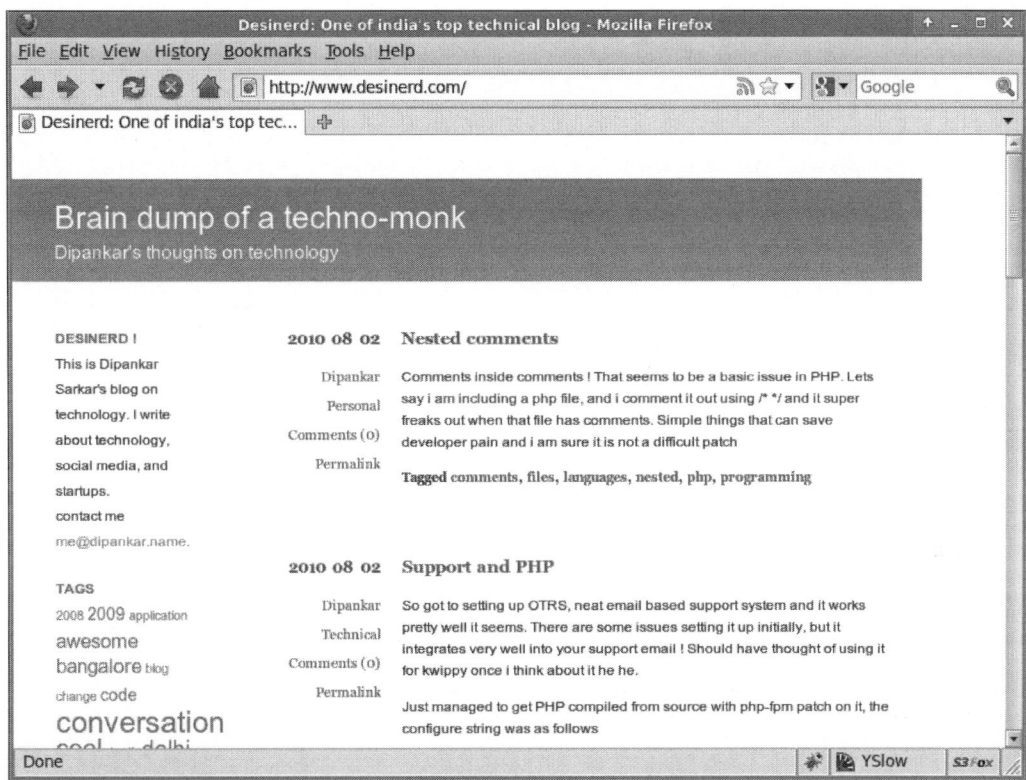

How to do it...

Let's try to set up a complete WordPress blog using Nginx and PHP over fcgi. In this recipe, you will end up learning the various details around the WordPress and Nginx stack.

1. Download WordPress - `http://Wordpress.org/latest.tar.gz`.

2. Untar it at `/var/www/www.example1.com/`:

   ```
   tar -xvzf latest.tar.gz
   ```

3. Add the following configuration in `Nginx.conf` within the http directive:

   ```
   server {
       listen        80;
       server_name   www.example1.com;
       root    /var/www/www.example1.com;
       index index.php index.html;
       try_files $uri $uri/ /index.php?q=$uri;
       location ~* \.(jpg|jpeg|gif|css|png|js|ico|html)$ {
           expires max;
   ```

```
    }
    location ~ \.php$ {
        include /etc/nginx/fastcgi_params;
        fastcgi_pass   127.0.0.1:9000;
    }
}
```

4. Restart the server:

```
kill -HUP <master PID>
```

5. Go to the blog, and start the installation.

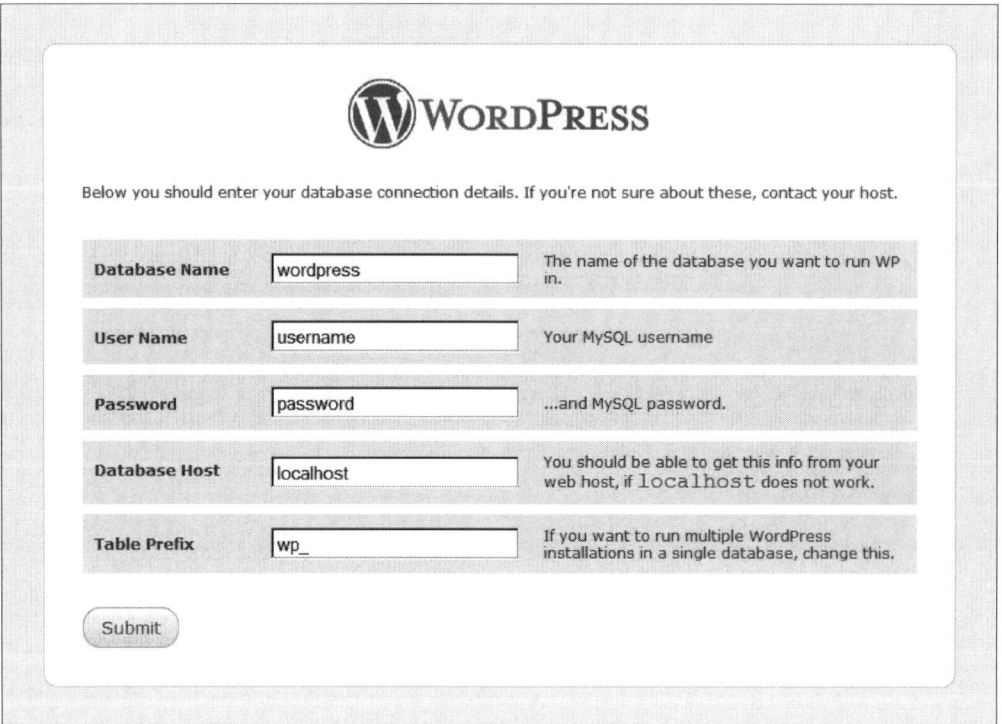

6. Log in to the administrative section and set up the clean URLs.

The following screenshot is the permalink setting that allows you to have clean URLs without `.php` with the various parameters appended. That makes it very search engine and human friendly:

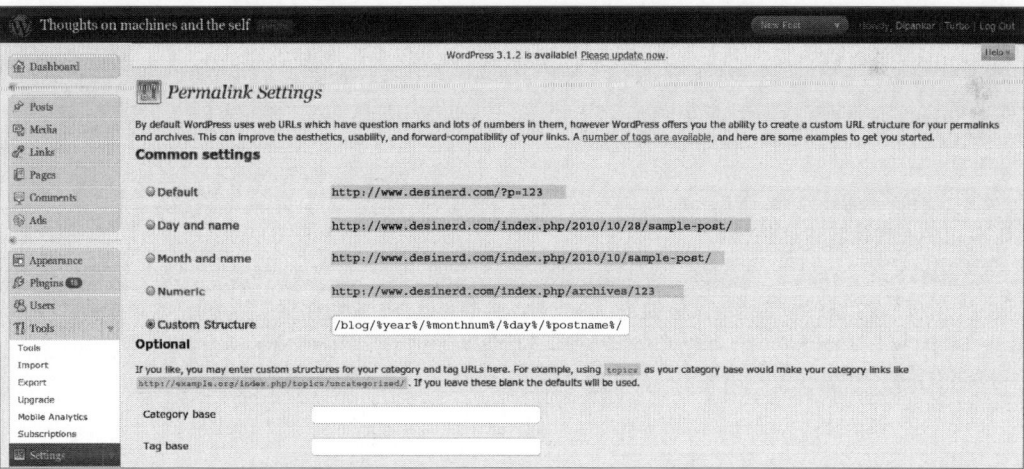

7. We are nearly done. Now you can go ahead and customize your cool, new WordPress blog!

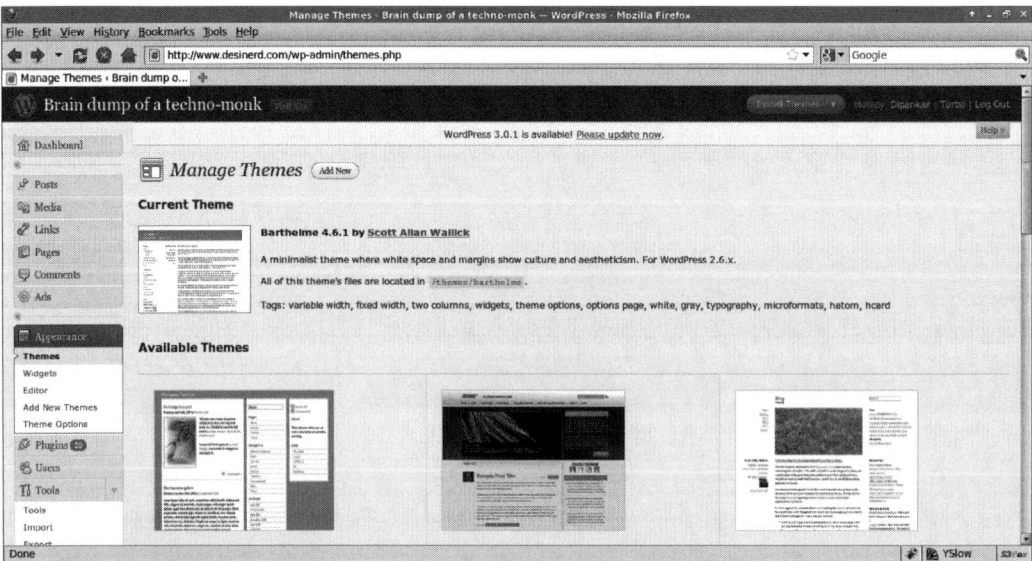

How it works...

This is a fairly basic setup. The clean URLs are handled by one rewrite. The interesting part is the static file serving, which is highlighted in the configuration above, that checks if the file being served is a static file (that is a GIF, PNG, DOC, and so on). If it is, then the file is served with an expiry header with long expiration time. This reduces the consumed bandwidth as it facilitates extended client side caching.

There's more...

Many sites have alternative setups to handle higher loads, and use plugins like `wp-supercache`. The following configuration has the correct rewrites for fully utilizing the combined power of `wp-supercache` and Nginx. This setup has the capability to handle a significant amount of load within very low resource constraints:

```
if (-f $request_filename) {
        break;
  }
set $supercache_file '';
set $supercache_uri $request_uri;
if ($request_method = POST) {
        set $supercache_uri '';
  }
```

```
    if ($query_string) {
            set $supercache_uri '';
    }
    if ($http_cookie ~* "comment_author_|Wordpress|wp-postpass_" )
{
            set $supercache_uri '';
    }
    if ($supercache_uri ~ ^(.+)$) {
            set $supercache_file /blog/wp-content/cache/
supercache/$http_host/$1index.html;
    }
    if (-f $document_root$supercache_file) {
            rewrite ^(.*)$ $supercache_file break;
    }
    if (!-e $request_filename) {
        rewrite ^(.+)$ /index.php?q=$1 last;
    }
```

In the following screenshot you can see the WP super cache Manager plugin configuration page which allows you to setup other parameters for the caching based on your site requirements. In the above example we handle the basic settings which assume that all the pages need to be cached.

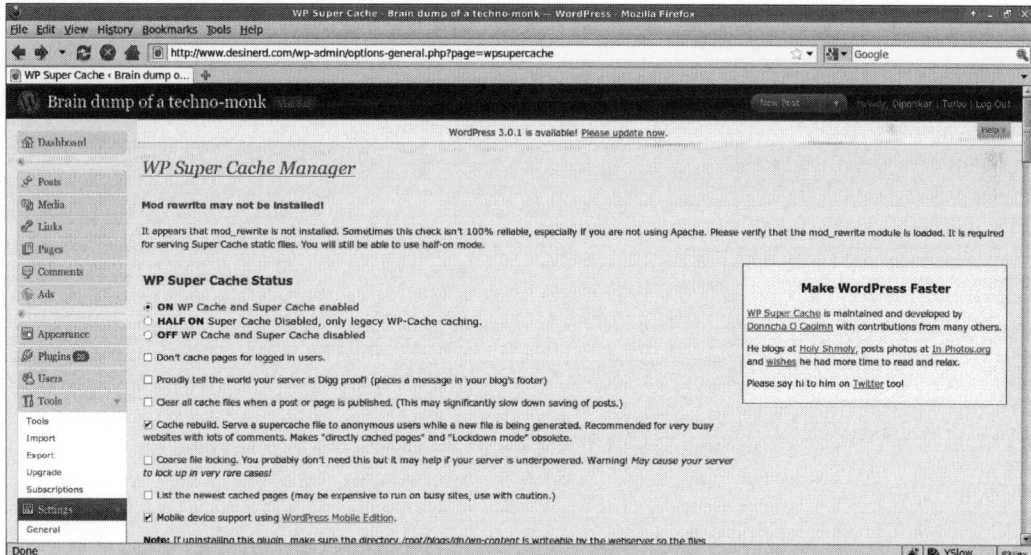

Setting up a Drupal site with static file serving

Drupal is an emerging open source CMS and has captured the imagination of many PHP developers and enthusiasts alike. In this recipe, we will have a look at how we can set up Drupal using Nginx and PHP over FastCGI.

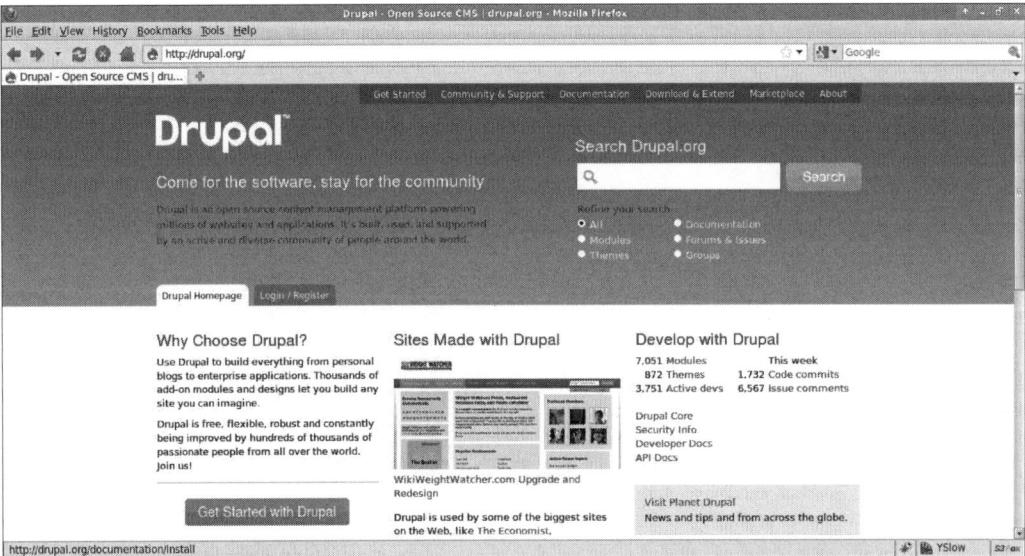

How to do it...

1. Download Drupal: `http://ftp.Drupal.org/files/projects/Drupal-6.19.tar.gz`

2. Untar Drupal to `/var/www/www.example1.com/`.

3. Add the following to your `Nginx.conf`:

```
server {
    listen        80;
    server_name   www.example1.com;
    root    /var/www/www.example1.com;
    index   index.php index.html index.htm
    try_files $uri $uri/ /index.php?q=$uri;
    location ~* \.(jpg|jpeg|gif|css|png|js|ico|html)$ {
        expires max;
    }
    location ~ \.php$ {
```

```
            include /etc/nginx/fastcgi_params;
            fastcgi_pass   127.0.0.1:9000;
        }
    }
```

4. Reload Nginx:

    kill -HUP <master PID>

5. Set up Drupal:

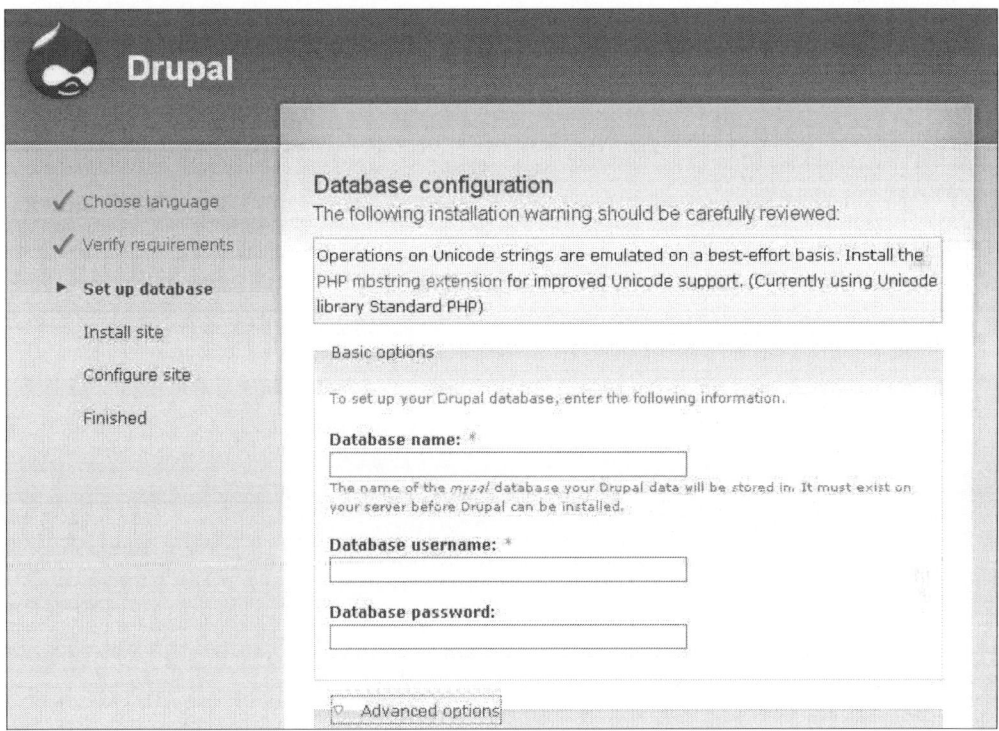

The preceding screenshot lets you set up the database settings for the installation. In the following screen, you will be logged in as administrator and will have the ability to manipulate the various options of the platform:

Welcome to your new Drupal website!

Please follow these steps to set up and start using your website:

1. **Configure your website**

   Once logged in, visit the administration section, where you can customize and configure all aspects of your website.

2. **Enable additional functionality**

   Next, visit the module list and enable features which suit your specific needs. You can find additional modules in the Drupal modules download section.

3. **Customize your website design**

   To change the "look and feel" of your website, visit the themes section. You may choose from one of the included themes or download additional themes from the Drupal themes download section.

4. **Start posting content**

   Finally, you can create content for your website. This message will disappear once you have promoted a post to the front page.

For more information, please refer to the help section, or the online Drupal handbooks. You may also post at the Drupal forum, or view the wide range of other support options available.

How it works...

The basic Drupal setup is very similar to the WordPress setup shown in the earlier recipe, and has the same rewrite rules. You need to transform the clean URL into a parameterized URL for `index.php`, as shown in the highlighted directive, `try_files`.

There's more...

Drupal has an exciting caching framework called Boost, which enhances the speed drastically. It can be used in conjunction with Nginx to handle fairly high loads. Do note that this stack with the boost modules has certain pitfalls when it comes to large Drupal sites; it is best utilized with smaller portals.

```
set $boost "";
if ( $request_method = GET ) {
set $boost G;
}
if ($http_cookie !~ "DRUPAL_UID") {
set $boost "${boost}D";
}
if ($query_string = "") {
set $boost "${boost}Q";
}
if ( -f $document_root/cache/$host/0/index.html ) {
set $boost "${boost}I";
}
if ($boost = GDQI) {
rewrite ^/$ /cache/$server_name/0/index.html break;
}
if ( -f $document_root/cache/$host/0$request_uri.html ) {
set $boost "${boost}F";
}
if ($boost = GDQIF) {
rewrite .? /cache/$server_name/0$request_uri.html break;
}
if ( -d $document_root/cache/$host/0$request_uri ) {
set $boost "${boost}E";
}
if ( -f $document_root/cache/$host/0$request_uri/index.html ) {
set $boost "${boost}F";
}
if ($boost = GDQEF) {
rewrite .? /cache/$server_name/0$request_uri/index.html break;
}
if (!-e $request_filename) {
rewrite ^/(.*)$ /index.php?q=$1 last;
}
```

The important assumption in the above case is that the boost cache is set at `/cache/`.

Boost cacheability settings (key=cacheability, weight=0)

☑ Cache pages that contain URL Variables (key=boost_cache_query, weight=0)
Boost will cache pages that end with "?page=1" among others (anything with a "?" in the url).

☑ Cache html documents/pages (key=boost_cache_html, weight=0)
Boost will cache most drupal pages.

☑ Cache .xml & /feed (key=boost_cache_xml, weight=0)
Boost will cache .xml and /feed urls as xml data.

☐ Cache ajax/json (key=boost_cache_json, weight=0)
Boost will cache ajax/json responses.

☑ Cache .css (key=boost_cache_css, weight=0)
Boost will cache CSS files.

☑ Cache .js (key=boost_cache_js, weight=0)
Boost will cache javascript files.

Statically cache specific pages (key=boost_cacheability_option, weight=0):

◉ Cache every page except the listed pages.

◯ Cache only the listed pages.

◯ Cache pages for which the following PHP code returns TRUE (PHP-mode, experts only).

Pages (key=boost_cacheability_pages, weight=0):

```

```

Enter one page per line as Drupal paths. The '*' character is a wild-card. Example paths are '*blog*' for the blog page and *blog*/* for every personal blog. *<front>* is the front page. If the PHP-mode is chosen, enter PHP code between <?*php* ?>. Note that executing incorrect PHP-code can severely break your Drupal site.

Setting up a Magento site with static file serving

Magento is a neat e-commerce CMS which has been around for a fair bit of time. It has gained widespread acceptance due to its strong API and committed developer community. In this recipe, we will have a look at how to set up Magento using Nginx and PHP over FastCGI.

How to do it...

1. Download Magento: `http://www.magentocommerce.com/getmagento/1.4.1.1/magento-1.4.1.1.zip`

2. Untar Magento to `/var/www/www.example1.com/`.

3. Add this to your `Nginx.conf`:

```
server {
    listen 80 default;
    server_name www.example1.com;
    root /var/www/www.example1.com;

    location / {
        index index.html index.php;
        if (!-e $request_filename) {
            rewrite / /index.php;
        }
    }
    location ~ \.php/ {
        rewrite ^(.*\.php)/ $1 last;
    }
    location ~ \.php$ {
        include         fastcgi_params;
        fastcgi_pass    127.0.0.1:9000;
```

```
        }
    }
```

4. Reload Nginx:

    ```
    kill -HUP <master PID>
    ```

5. Install Magento:

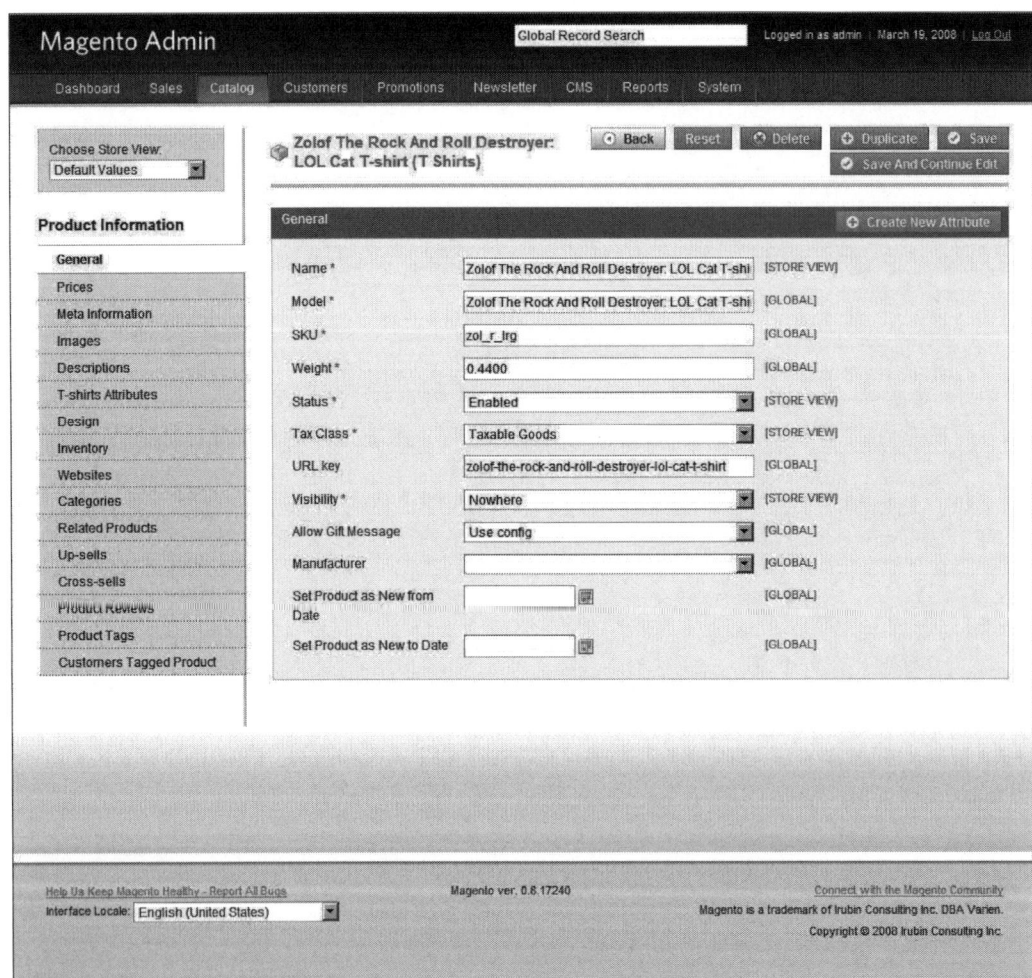

How it works...

Magento, unlike Drupal or WordPress, does not rewrite its URL to `index.php`. All the pages map to `index.php`. This is achieved by the rewrite rule that has been highlighted in the configuration code above.

Converting your Apache's .htaccess into Nginx rewrites

One of the primary uses of Nginx rewrites is to help you easily translate Apache2's .htaccess to usable Nginx configuration. Apache2 is the dominant open source web server in the world. In such a situation, inevitably most of the code available has .htaccess rules and very little direction regarding how to go about configuring Nginx rewrites so that it can properly run the site.

How to do it...

In this we will have a look at an example where we take an .htaccess file and see its equivalent Nginx rewrite rules. In the later sections, we will have a look at some patterns that emerge out of the conversion which you can later utilize for converting other scripts.

```
Options -Indexes
Options +FollowSymLinks

# Enable ETag
#FileETag MTime Size
FileETag none

# Set expiration header
ExpiresActive on
ExpiresDefault A2592000
Header append Cache-Control "public"

# Compress some text file types
AddOutputFilterByType DEFLATE text/html text/plain text/css text/
xml application/x-javascript text/javascript application/javascript
application/json

# Deactivate compression for buggy browsers
BrowserMatch ^Mozilla/4 gzip-only-text/html
BrowserMatch ^Mozilla/4\.0[678] no-gzip
BrowserMatch \bMSIE !no-gzip !gzip-only-text/html

# Set header information for proxies
Header append Vary User-Agent

#######################################################
# Rewrite Rules
#######################################################

RewriteEngine on

# Require SSL (HTTPS) on the signup page
RewriteCond %{SERVER_PORT} 80
RewriteCond %{REQUEST_URI} ^/signup/?
RewriteRule ^(.*)$ https://www.example.com/$1 [R,L]
```

```
# Redirect /signup/plan or /signup/plan/ -> /signup/index.
php?account_type=plan
RewriteRule ^signup/([A-Za-z]+)/?$ /signup/index.php?account_type=$1
[NC,L]

# Redirect /home/123 or /home/123/ -> home.php?home_id=123
RewriteRule ^home/([0-9]+)/?$ home.php?home_id=$1 [NC,L]

# Redirect /homes/ in case someone made a typo when it should have
been /home/
RewriteRule ^homes/([0-9]+)/?$ home.php?home_id=$1 [NC,L]

##################################################
# Default Settings
##################################################

# hide apache server signaute on apache generated pages (e.g. 404)
ServerSignature Off
```

The equivalent Nginx rule set is:

```
if ($server_port ~ "80"){
 set $rule_0 1$rule_0;
}
if ($uri ~ "^/signup/?"){
 set $rule_0 2$rule_0;
}
if ($rule_0 = "21"){
 rewrite ^/(.*)$ https://www.example.com/$1 redirect;
 break;
}
 rewrite ^/signup/([A-Za-z]+)/?$ /signup/index.php?account_type=$1
last;
 rewrite ^/home/([0-9]+)/?$ /home.php?home_id=$1 last;
 rewrite ^/homes/([0-9]+)/?$ /home.php?home_id=$1 last;
```

How it works...

Now let's have a look at how exactly the rules have got translated, so the Apache rewrite rules basically enforce the following rules:

  ▶ If the request is on port 80 and the URL is /signup/ then it is rewritten to the HTTPS version

  ▶ It redirects all /signup/plan or /signup/plan/ to /signup/index. php?account_type=plan

  ▶ It redirects all /home/123 or /home/123/ to home.php?home_id=123

  ▶ It fixes all /homes/ to /home/

So basically, if you notice, the conversion is very direct and rather simple. The Apache .htaccess basically utilizes a sequential set of conditions which are converted to if conditionals statements in Nginx which manipulate some variables. The following table gives you a clearer look at the direct conversion of the rewrites.

Apache	Nginx	Notes

RewriteCond %{SERVER_PORT} 80	if ($server_port ~ "80"){
	 set $rule_0 1$rule_0;
	 }
		This is a simple rewrite conditional check for what is the server port.

RewriteCond %{REQUEST_URI} ^/signup/?	if ($uri ~ "^/signup/?"){
	 set $rule_0 2$rule_0;
	 }
		This is a check for the URL structure.

RewriteRule ^(.*)$ https:// www.example.com/$1 [R,L]	if ($rule_0 = "21"){
	 rewrite ^/(.*)$ https:// www.example.com/$1 redirect;
	 break;
	 }
		This Rule is fired only when the above two conditions are met. It's a redirect as specified by the R in the Apache configuration and redirect in Nginx.

RewriteRule ^signup/ ([A-Za-z]+)/?$ /signup/index. php?account_type=$1 [NC,L]	rewrite ^/signup/ ([A-Za-z]+)/?$ /signup/ index.php?account_ type=$1 last;	This simply matches URLs which look like /signup/something and rewrites them to /signup/index. php?account_type=something . If you notice, something can contain alphabets to have a match.
RewriteRule ^home/([0-9]+)/?$ home.php?home_ id=$1 [NC,L]	rewrite ^/home/ ([0-9]+)/?$ /home. php?home_id=$1 last;	This is similar to the above rewrite and matched for a number.
RewriteRule ^homes/([0-9]+)/?$ home.php?home_ id=$1 [NC,L]	rewrite ^/homes/ ([0-9]+)/?$ /home. php?home_id=$1 last;	This rewrite is matches for patterns like /homes/123, / homes/123123 and so on. It is similar to the above rewrites.

It is clear how you can take rewrite conditionals in Apache htaccess, and convert them to Nginx conditions which modify the value of a variable as shown in the comparison above. It is fairly simple to see the pattern of conversion for the actual rewrites that take place by looking at the table above.

There's more...

Today, there are a lot of online tools that are fairly advanced and let you convert your .htaccess file directly into an Nginx configuration! Though it is still safe to assume that more efficient code is generated by human conversion in slightly complex cases. You can try using `http://www.anilcetin.com/convert-apache-htaccess-to-nginx/` and see your Apache configuration converted into Nginx configuration with one click.

Using maps to make configurations cleaner

There is a very useful Nginx module that allows the classification of set of values into different sets of values, which is then stored in a variable. The idea is that it makes it much simpler to write switch-case, like statements where you have a different rewrite when there is a different value. So let us look at some examples where the map module is effectively used.

How to do it...

Let's say you want to detect the incoming hostname and want to do something different on certain domains and sub-domains, we will write a map and utilize it in a simple rewrite rule:

```
map    $http_host   $name  {
  hostnames;
  default            0;
  example.com        1;
  *.example.com      1;
  test.com           2;
  *.test.com         2;
  .site.com          3;
}
if($name ~* 1) {
<some rewrite rule>
}
```

How it works...

This idea is simple. Here you have taken the `$http_host` variable and created a map where it will simply fill $name with the value corresponding to the matched value. So for example, if the site visited was `http://abc.site.com` then the $name value would be set at three as per the map.

The hostname directive allows you to write one instead of two mappings if you want to cover a complete domain, that is:

```
.example1.com        1;
```

Instead of:

```
example1.com         1;
*.example1.com       1;
```

There's more...

After this variable is mapped, one can utilize this for triggering other rewrite rules. The recipe for using cookies with rewrite rules could have potentially utilized this approach to have a much cleaner configuration file:

```
if ($cookie_env ~* "testing") {
        rewrite ^(.*)$   /testing/$1;
}
 if ($cookie_env ~* "staging") {
        rewrite ^(.*)$   /staging/$1;
}
 if ($cookie_env ~* "production") {
            rewrite ^(.*)$   /production/$1;
}
```

The above can be simply translated into:

```
map $cookie_env $type {
    default    /production/;
    testing    /testing/;
    staging    /staging/;
    production    /production/;
}
rewrite ^(.*)$   $type/$1;
```

This looks much cleaner and effectively is the equivalent to the configuration that is not using the Map module.

3
Get It All Logged: The Logging Module

In this chapter, we will cover:

- ► Setting up error log path and levels
- ► Logging it like Apache
- ► Disabling logging of 404 in error logs
- ► Using different logging profiles in the same setup
- ► Enabling a log file cache
- ► Utilizing separate error logs per virtual host
- ► Setting up log rotation
- ► Enabling remote logging with syslog-ng
- ► Setting up your custom logs for easy parsing

Introduction

This chapter aims to teach the basics as well as the advanced configurations that can be done around the Nginx logging module, like log management, backup, rotation, and more. Logging is very crucial as it can help you identify and track various attributes of your application, like performance, user behavior, and much more. It also helps you as a system administrator to identify, both reactively and proactively, potential security issues.

Setting up error log path and levels

The basic configurations that one needs to get the logging modules working properly are setting up the location of the logging files and configuring the level of the logging that will take place.

Nginx allows a clear separation of the access and the error logs, thus letting you easily track your error lists.

How to do it...

You can use the following configuration to setup a file path for logging in addition to setting the format in which to log in:

```
http {
log_format combined '$remote_addr - $remote_user [$time_local]  '
                    '"$request" $status $body_bytes_sent '
                    '"$http_referer" "$http_user_agent"';

access_log  /var/log/nginx/access.log combined;
error_log /var/log/nginx/error.log crit;
. . .
```

How it works...

This simple configuration will allow us to log the various HTTP activities that occur on all the sites hosted in the particular environment. Here is a sample log from the access log:

```
204.15.240.18 - - [11/Nov/2010:10:57:50 -0800] "GET /public/images-
redux/infobox_join_type.png HTTP/1.1" 200 10212 "http://example.com/
public/css/style-redux.css" "Mozilla/5.0 (Windows; U; Windows NT 5.1;
en-US; rv:1.9.2.10) Gecko/20100914 Firefox/3.6.10"
```

It is easy to see how the various variables are outputted in order, as defined with the combined format.

The error log, which is now logged at `/var/log/nginx/error.log`, will start logging all the critical errors, and here is a sample entry from an error log:

```
2010/11/11 10:07:28 [error] 3172#0: accept() failed (53: Software
caused connection abort)
2010/11/11 10:15:12 [error] 3175#0: *136332 open() "/root/sites/
app/public/images/fancybox/blank.gif" failed (2: No such file or
directory), client: 122.176.248.115, server: example1.com, request:
"GET /public/images/fancybox/blank.gif HTTP/1.1", host: "example1.
com", referrer: "http://example1.com/"
```

There's more...

You can change the level of error logging (`error_log`) to `debug`, `info`, `notice`, `warn`, `error`, `crit`, or `alert`, based upon your application needs. It is usually best to try out the various levels to understand what exactly it outputs, and weather that can satisfy your current debugging needs.

Error level	What does it mean?
Alert	Emergency conditions
Crit	Critical conditions
Error	Error conditions
Warn	Warning conditions
Notice	Normal, but significant conditions
Info	Information messages
Debug	Debug-level messages

Logging it like Apache

Apache or httpd is the most used open source web server out there. It has a very stable codebase and community which has made it more or less the standard for open source enterprise applications out there.

Most of the log analyzers are configured with Apache logging format in mind. Our goal in this recipe is to enable us to use log analyzing tools which already work well with Apache in our Nginx setup.

How to do it...

If you want the log to look like the Apache logs, you will need to enter the following code:

```
log_format main '$remote_addr - $remote_user [$time_local] '
                '"$request" $status $body_bytes_sent "$http_referer" '
                '"$http_user_agent" "$http_x_forwarded_for"';

access_log /var/log/nginx/access.log main;
```

How it works...

In this, we basically create a new Apache compatible format which will be easily read with tools like AWStats. We then set the standard as the Nginx access log format in the preceding configuration. The format has the following fields:

Variable	What is it?
$remote_addr	This is the IP of the remote address that was accessing the site.
$remote_user	If the user is logged in with HTTP authentication, this would be their username.
$time_local	This is the local timestamp of the server when the request was made.
$request	The request that was made on the server.
$status	The HTTP response code (200, 404, 500, and so on).
$body_bytes_sent	This is the size of the response that was sent to the server.
$http_referer	This is the site from where the user has arrived on to this particular page/made this HTTP request.
$http_user_agent	This is the browser type that was used to make this HTTP request.
$http_x_forwarded_for	If the server is running as a reverse proxy then this will display the actual IP of the server.

```
66.249.64.13 - - [18/Sep/2004:11:07:48 +1000] "GET /robots.txt
HTTP/1.0" 200 468 "-" "Googlebot/2.1"
66.249.64.13 - - [18/Sep/2004:11:07:48 +1000] "GET / HTTP/1.0" 200
6433 "-" "Googlebot/2.1"
```

The preceding lines from the access log display the format in action. This particular format will easily work with all the web log parsing and analyzing tools, such as webalizer and AWStats, with no changes at all.

Disabling logging of 404 in error logs

In the age of Google, we can see that there are thousands of crawlers out there trying to get the most out of your site and content by reading through all your pages. In a lot of situations, when you update or upgrade a site, these crawlers start to take up system resources by trying to access pages that used to exist and do not anymore. This also increases the system overheads of logging and can potentially become a bottleneck for your site. This recipe will address this particular issue.

How to do it...

This piece of configuration is placed in the location context of the configuration, as shown in the following code:

```
location = /robots.txt {
   log_not_found  off;
}
```

How it works...

This simple configuration will not log when the /robots.txt file is not found on the server. This will save the unnecessary overhead of opening the error log file and writing out an 404 entry indicating that the file, robots.txt(cit) is being found.

Using different logging profiles in the same setup

As we have seen before, Nginx allows you to easily set up a logging format. In this recipe, we will explore how one configuration file can exploit multiple logging formats. This neat functionality can help you generate custom logs specific to a particular section of the site whenever necessary.

How to do it...

This particular configuration will implement three logging formats and then effectively utilize them for logging different sections of the site:

```
http {

log_format main '$remote_addr - $remote_user [$time_local] '
                '"$request" $status $body_bytes_sent "$http_referer" '
                '"$http_user_agent" "$http_x_forwarded_for"';

# You do not need HTTP authentication information and Refer
information for the static files !
log_format static_main '$remote_addr [$time_local] '
                '"$request" $status $body_bytes_sent
                '"$http_user_agent";

# You do not need to know about the bytes sent in an error logging
case
log_format error_main '$remote_addr - $remote_user [$time_local] '
                '"$request" $status "$http_user_agent";

. . .
```

```
server {
    listen 80;
    server_name example1.com;
    error_log var/log/nginx/example1_error.log error_main;
    location / {
        ...
        access_log /var/log/nginx/example1_main.log main;
    }
location /static/ {
        ...
        access_log /var/log/nginx/example1_static.log static_main;
    }
}

...

}
```

How it works...

The `main` log format will be used to log the normal dynamic PHP request, while the `static_main` log format is being used to log the static requests that come to Nginx. Finally we use an `error_main` format to keep track of the errors.

There's more...

You have access to the following variables to use in the `log_format` structure. These can be utilized effectively to gather and understand whatever Nginx can access in your stack:

Variable	Description
$arg_PARAMETER	This variable contains the value of the GET request variable PARAMETER if present in the query string.
$args	This variable is the GET parameter's in request line, for example, `foo=123&bar=blahblah`.
$binary_remote_addr	The address of the client in binary form.
$body_bytes_sent	The bytes of the body sent.
$content_length	This variable is equal to line Content-Length in the header of request.
$content_type	This variable is equal to line Content-Type in the header of request.
$document_root	This variable is equal to the value of directive root for the current request.

Variable	Description
`$document_uri`	The same as `$uri`.
`$host`	This variable is equal to line Host in the header of request or name of the server processing the request if the Host header is not available. This variable may have a different value from `$http_host` when the Host input header is absent or has an empty value.
`$http_HEADER`	The value of the HTTP header HEADER when converted to lowercase and with "dashes" converted to "underscores", for example, `$http_user_agent`, `$http_referer`.
`$is_args`	Evaluates to "?" if `$args` is set, returns "" otherwise.
`$request_uri`	This variable is equal to the *original* request URI as received from the client including the args. It cannot be modified. Look at `$uri` for the post-rewrite/altered URI. Does not include host name. Example: `"/foo/bar.php?arg=baz"`.
`$scheme`	The HTTP scheme (that is http, https). Evaluated only on demand, for example: `rewrite ^(.+)$ $scheme://example.com$1 redirect;`
`$server_addr`	Equal to the server address. As a rule, for obtaining the value of this variable is done one system call. In order to avoid system call, it is necessary to indicate addresses in directives, listen, and to use parameter bind.
`$server_name`	The name of the server.
`$server_port`	This variable is equal to the port of the server, to which the request arrived.
`$server_protocol`	This variable is equal to the protocol of request, usually this HTTP/1.0 or HTTP/1.1.
`$uri`	This variable is equal to current URI in the request (without arguments, those are in `$args`.) It can differ from `$request_uri` which is what is sent by the browser. Examples of how it can be modified are internal redirects, or with the use of index. Does not include host name. Example: `"/foo/bar.html"`.

Enabling a log file cache

Logging is primarily a disk based activity, and on a busy server, that requires logging as an audit requirement. It is crucial to ensure that you enable file descriptor caching in Nginx. This is a performance enhancement recipe that will also increase the life of your server hard drive.

How to do it...

You can put this configuration in the `http` part of the configuration:

```
http {
...
open_log_file_cache max=1000 inactive=20s min_uses=2 valid=1m;
..
```

How it works...

This simple configuration sets up the following flags which are described in the following table:

Flag	Utility
Max	Maximal number of descriptors in the cache, with overflow Least Recently Used removed (LRU)
Inactive	Sets the time after which descriptor without hits during this time are removed; default is 10 seconds
min_uses	Sets the minimum number of file usage within the time specified in parameter inactive, after which the file descriptor will be put in the cache; default is 1
Valid	Sets the time until it will be checked if file still exists under same name; default is 60 seconds
Off	Disables the cache

These settings can be optimized over some span of testing, thus giving you the best of what Nginx has to offer with logging and reducing your performance overheads for the same.

Utilizing separate error logs per virtual host

We looked earlier at how simple it is in Nginx to set up virtual hosts and manage them clearly in their separate files. In this recipe, we are going to have a look at how we create different access and error logs for each virtual host.

How to do it...

This is a configuration that takes three virtual hosts (`www.example1.com`, `www.example2.com`, and `www.example3.com`) which have different access and error logs:

```
http {
...
server {
```

```
    listen 80;
    server_name www.example1.com ;
    access_log /var/log/nginx/example1.access.log;
    error_log /var/log/nginx/example1.error.log;
    ...
}
server {
    listen 80;
    server_name www.example2.com ;
    access_log /var/log/nginx/example2.access.log;
    error_log /var/log/nginx/example2.error.log;
    ...
}
server {
    listen 80;
    server_name www.example3.com ;
    access_log /var/log/nginx/example3.access.log;
    error_log /var/log/nginx/example3.error.log;
    ...
}
}
```

How it works...

As you can see, we can place `access_log` and `error_log` directives individually in each of the virtual host configurations. This allows us to create different files for each of those sites.

There's more...

You can potentially combine the earlier recipe of different log formats and this recipe to create different kinds of access and error logs for each of your sites. This clearly exhibits the immense power that the Nginx logging module brings to the table for the system administrators.

```
http {
...
server {
    listen 80;
    server_name www.example1.com ;
    access_log /var/log/nginx/example1.access.log main;
    error_log /var/log/nginx/example1.error.log error_main;
    ...
}
```

The preceding example shows how we are logging the access and error logs with different formats, which are `main` and `error_main` respectively. This may be necessary in cases where one logs fewer variables for the access logs purposes and more esoteric variables to track errors in the error logs.

Setting up log rotation

In production sites that have been running for a decent amount of time, log archiving becomes a necessity. For proper log archiving, you will need to have a proper log rotation system in place. Every website request generates more than one log entry (as there are logging for the static files as well), so logs tend to bloat up quickly. This recipe helps you tackle the log rotation setup with Nginx, making sure you are archiving your logs correctly.

This depends on the logrotate script that is available, for example, on both Fedora and Debian distributions.

How to do it...

You will need to add a configuration to the logrotate conf file:

```
/var/log/nginx/*.log {
        daily
        missingok
        rotate 52
        compress
        delaycompress
        notifempty
        create 640 root adm
        sharedscripts
        postrotate
                [ ! -f /var/run/nginx.pid ] || kill -USR1 `cat
/var/run/nginx.pid`
        endscript
}
```

This assumes that the Nginx configurations are placed in the `/var/log/nginx` directory and the Nginx PID file exists at `/var/run/nginx.pid`.

How it works...

This is a simple configuration for logrotate which effectively carries out the following steps:

1. Moves the existing log file with a new filename and compresses it.

2. Makes a USR1 signal call to the Nginx master process, which releases the log which has just been moved and starts writing into a normal log file.

The logrotate script allows very interesting configurations which allow you great control over when the log needs to be rotated, what compressions you need, and with what permissions the files to be archived.

Enabling remote logging with syslog-ng

Imagine running a cluster of servers spread out over various geographies. In such a scenario, one will probably need to do remote logging on a set of redundant central logging servers. It makes life easier for log parsing and system administration tasks as well.

In this recipe, we will have a look at syslog-ng and Nginx to get them working together in a networked environment. This will involve some interesting things, like patching the Nginx codebase.

How to do it...

If you want to get the Nginx installation to interact with syslog-ng, you will need to carry out the following steps carefully. This recipe assumes that you have already installed syslog-ng on your system:

1. You will need to download Nginx from the following URL: (http://nginx.org/download/nginx-0.7.67.tar.gz)

   ```
   wget http://nginx.org/download/nginx-0.7.67.tar.gz
   ```

2. Then untar the downloaded file:

   ```
   tar -xvzf nginx-0.7.67.tar.gz
   ```

3. Download the patch: (http://bugs.gentoo.org/attachment.cgi?id=197180)

   ```
   wget "http://bugs.gentoo.org/attachment.cgi?id=197180"  -O syslog.patch
   ```

4. Apply the patch:

   ```
   patch -p0 < syslog.patch
   ```

5. Configure Nginx:

   ```
   ./configure --with-syslog
   ```

6. Build and install Nginx:

   ```
   make && make install
   ```

7. You will now need to configure the syslog client, adding the following configuration to `/etc/syslog-ng/syslog-ng.conf` and restarting the syslog-ng service:

```
filter f_local5 { facility(local5); };
destination d_loghost {tcp("nginx_log" port(514));};
log { source(s_all); filter(f_local5); destination(d_loghost); };
```

8. You will now need to configure the remote logging server `nginx_log`, adding the following configuration to `/etc/syslog-ng/syslog-ng.conf` and restarting the syslog-ng service:

```
source s_remote { tcp(); };
destination d_clients { file("/var/log/HOSTS/nginx.$HOST"); };
log { source(s_remote); destination(d_clients); };
```

9. You can test this configuration out by running the following:

```
logger -p local5.info HelloWorld
```

How it works...

Nginx, by default, does not support syslog-ng and needs some patching to work correctly. So in the first set of steps we actually install Nginx with the patch and then proceed to configure syslog-ng.

There are two parts to the syslog-ng configuration. In the first we actually configure the client on which Nginx is running and make the local5 facility (where Nginx logs in our case) point to the syslog-ng server running on the `nginx_log` server. The second part involved configuring the syslog-ng server to accept log request from the remote client and putting them at certain locations on the hard drive.

There is a small utility called "logger", which allows you to test out the logging on your machine without invoking Nginx. It's pretty nifty and lets you easily debug your syslog-ng setup.

Setting up your custom logs for easy parsing

The point of logging is not only to find out errors in a setup, but also for various analytics that one can perform on the usage of the sites running on the server. There are various tools that are available that one can use to analyze your web logs. Some of the open source and freely available ones are AWstats, webalizer, and so on. We will have a look at how to set up for AWstats.

The following screenshot is a sample of the AWstats generated HTML report:

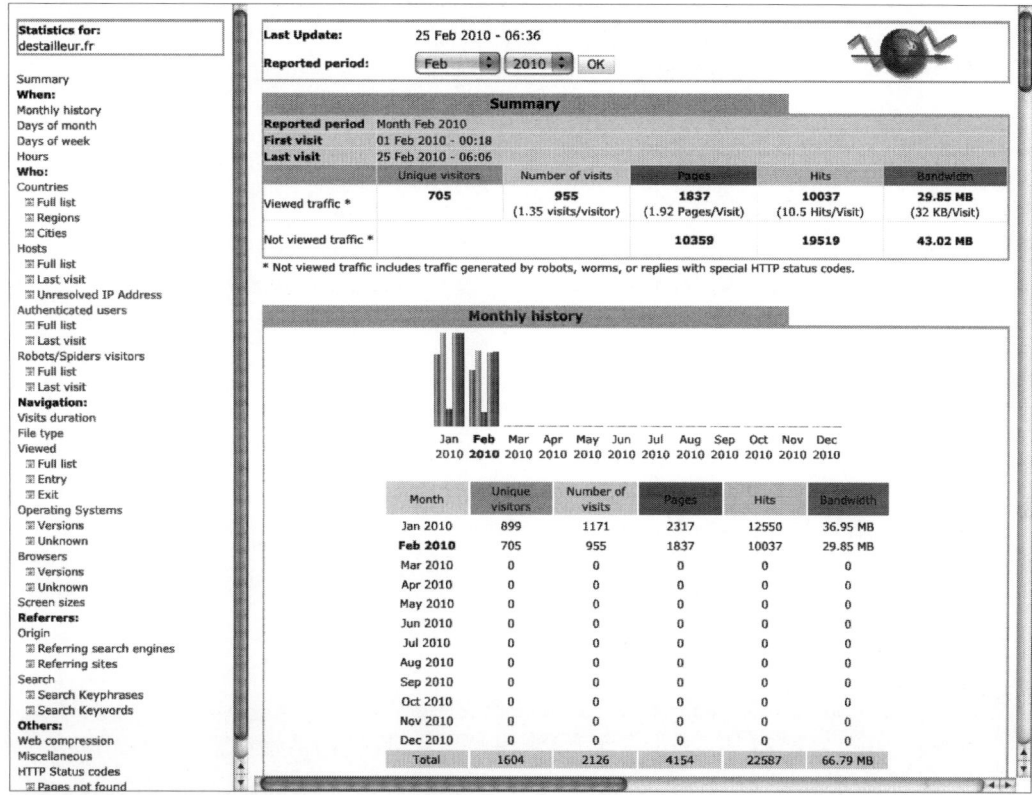

How to do it...

We will first have a look at how to install AWstats, and then configure it to create a continuous report around Nginx logs.

1. Add the following to the Nginx configuration file:

```
log_format  new_log
$remote_addr - $remote_user [$time_local] $request '
      '"$status" $body_bytes_sent "$http_referer" '
      '"$http_user_agent" "$http_x_forwarded_for"';
access_log  logs/access.log new_log;
```

2. Now we need to install the AWstats package, so download the latest version and then run the configuration wizard `awstats_configure.pl` to create a new statistics profile:

```
-----> Check for web server install

Enter full config file path of your Web server.
Example: /etc/httpd/httpd.conf
Example: /usr/local/apache2/conf/httpd.conf
Example: c:Program filesapache groupapacheconfhttpd.conf
Config file path ('none' to skip web server setup):
#> none
Enter
Your web server config file(s) could not be found.
You will need to setup your web server manually to declare AWStats
script as a CGI, if you want to build reports dynamically.
See AWStats setup documentation (file docs/index.html)

-----> Update model config file '/usr/local/awstats/wwwroot/cgi-
bin/awstats.model.conf'
   File awstats.model.conf updated.

-----> Need to create a new config file ?
Do you want me to build a new AWStats config/profile
file (required if first install) [y/N] ?
#> y
Enter
-----> Define config file name to create
What is the name of your web site or profile analysis ?
Example: www.mysite.com
Example: demo
Your web site, virtual server or profile name:
#> www.example1.com
www.example1.com
Enter
-----> Define config file path
In which directory do you plan to store your config file(s) ?
Default: /etc/awstats
Directory path to store config file(s) (Enter for default):
```

```
#>
----> Add update process inside a scheduler
Sorry, configure.pl does not support automatic add to cron yet.
You can do it manually by adding the following command to your
cron:
/usr/local/awstats/wwwroot/cgi-bin/awstats.pl -update -config=www.
moabc.net
Or if you have several config files and prefer having only one
command:
/usr/local/awstats/tools/awstats_updateall.pl now

A SIMPLE config file has been created: /etc/awstats/awstats.www.
example1.com.conf
You should have a look inside to check and change manually main
parameters.
You can then manually update your statistics for 'www.example1.
com' with command:
> perl awstats.pl -update -config=www.example1.com
You can also build static report pages for 'www.example1.com' with
command:
> perl awstats.pl -output=pagetype -config=www.example1.com

Press ENTER to finish...
```

3. You can now open the file generated /etc/awstats/awstats.www.example1.
   com.conf and update the LogFile variable to the path of the Nginx log file (assuming
   that they are being log rotated).

   ```
   LogFile="/usr/local/nginx/logs/access_%YYYY-0%MM-0%DD-0.log"
   ```

4. Now you can test out the new log analysis by using the following command. This will
   also depend on where you installed the AWstats package:

   ```
   /usr/local/awstats/wwwroot/cgi-bin/awstats.pl -update -config=www.
   example1.com
   ```

5. Now you need to generate the reports in HTML, so you will need to create a directory
   and then run the HTML generation script:

   ```
   # mkdir   /data/webroot/awstats

   # /usr/local/awstats/tools/awstats_buildstaticpages.pl -update

   -config=www.example1.com -lang=en -dir=/data/admin_web/awstats

   -awstatsprog=/usr/local/awstats/wwwroot/cgi-bin/awstats.pl
   ```

6. You can now add some configuration to Nginx to expose this HTML analysis on your own domain:

```
location ~ ^/awstats/ {
        root    /data/webroot/awstats;
        index   index.html;
        access_log off;
        error_log off;
        charset utf-8;
}
```

7. Now you can visit `http://example1.com/awstats/awstats.www.example1.com.html` to see the resultant HTML.

How it works...

This is a fairly simple setup, where we are initially setting up the logging format on Nginx so that we are able to fully exploit all that AWstats can generate for us. Then we go on to install AWstats, which is a set of Perl scripts. We generate a configuration for our domain `www.example1.com` and then start analyzing the log. In addition to the basic analysis, we can also generate really easy-to-use HTML reports.

There's more...

A tool like AWstats allows you to track things like:

- Visits (the number of unique visitors)
- Access time and the last visit
- User authentication (last time logged in using site credentials)
- Weekly peak time (the number of pages, click-through rate per hour, and week kilobytes)
- Name/country hosts visitors (pages, click-through rate, byte, 269 domains/ countries detected, GeoIP detection)
- Host list of recently visited and did not resolve the IP address list
- Most read entry and exit pages
- File types
- Site compression tables (mod_gzip or mod_deflate)
- Operating system (one for each operating system, the number of pages, click-through rate, byte, 35 OS detected)
- Type of browsers used
- Robot visits (319 robots detected)

- ▶ Worm attacks (5 worm family)
- ▶ Search engines statistics about what keywords lead users to your site
- ▶ HTTP protocol error (the most recent inspection did not find the page)
- ▶ Other reports based on the personalized URL and link parameters, involving the field of integrated marketing purpose
- ▶ Your site by adding "favorite bookmarks" views
- ▶ Screen size (in the index page of the need to add some HTML tags)
- ▶ The proportion of browser support: Java, Flash, RealG2 reader, Quicktime reader, WMA reader, PDF reader
- ▶ The ratio of load-balancing server cluster report

The preceding setup was not completely automated after you run the script for the first time. We can take a step ahead and put all this in a cron script that will help us run it as a cron job.

You will need to add the following in your cron (`crontab -e`):

```
00 1 * * * /usr/local/awstats/tools/awstats_buildstaticpages.pl
-update -config=www.example1.com -lang=cn -dir=/data/admin_web/awstats
-awstatsprog=/usr/local/awstats/wwwroot/cgi-bin/awstats.pl
```

This above cron job basically fires up a script every day at 1:00AM. The job of the script is to parse and generate the reports for the sites that it is configured for.

4
Slow Them Down: Access and Rate Limiting Module

In this chapter, we will cover:

- ► Limiting requests for any given session
- ► Blocking and allowing access using IP
- ► Setting up simple rate limiting for a download directory
- ► Rate limiting search engine bots
- ► Setting up GeoIP using the MaxMind country database
- ► Using the GeoIP module to set up access and rate control

Introduction

In this day and age of the Internet, the user is extremely sensitive about the quality of service they get from their online services. There are a lot of small companies with few resources that are able to capture a part of the market by innovating rapidly. Such companies eventually have to rate limit, as inevitably they have more traffic than their servers can handle.

Something as simple as getting "digged" (http://www.digg.com) or "slashdotted" (http://www.slashdot.org) used to bring down sites, but Nginx provides good protection against situations like this by providing rate limiting and server access based on IP.

Limiting requests for any given session

Due to its event driven nature, Nginx is being adopted all over the world whenever one needs performance with resource constraints. However, in a lot of situations, that is not enough and the only way is to limit request to ensure that your site is up and your server does not suffer any downtime.

How to do it...

The following configuration, when applied within a server directive, allows you to limit requests for a given session:

```
http {

limit_req_zone  $binary_remote_addr  zone=one:10m  rate=1r/s;

...

Server {
    limit_req   zone=one  burst=5;

...
}
```

How it works...

The `limit_req_zone` directive basically allows you to define what variable (in this case `$binary_remote_addr`) to act as the key of the sessions, in addition to allocating 10MB for this "zone" and limiting the rate to one request per second. There are no limits to the number of zones one can set up, as long as you have the memory to handle the zone allocations. A given zone which uses, say, the remote address as the key for the session, will be able to handle about 32,000 sessions in 1M of session memory allocated to it.

In the `server` directive, we actually do the request rate limiting by using the `limit_req` `directive`, which basically uses zone one, which allows no more than an average of one request per second with a maximum burst rate of five requests.

Any request that is beyond the rate capacity will receive a "Service unavailable" 503 error page.

There's more...

You can use other variables to act as the session key, but it is important to note that the session key variable size must be small to accommodate all the incoming connections (that is total connections x session value size < size of session cache).

Blocking and allowing access using IP

One of the most important things that a site needs to do is to blacklist some malicious IPs that over time try to probe and cause harm to your site. This can be done at multiple levels like the router, and even at the software firewall level which will also drive away this unnecessary load from Nginx. If you do not have enough control on your stack, then Nginx is the best place to start blocking those bots and hackers.

How to do it...

This lets you block some IPs from accessing your site:

```
server {
listen 80;
server_name www.example1.com;
location / {
  deny     192.168.1.1;
  allow    192.168.1.0/24;
  deny     all;
}
...
}
```

How it works...

It is clear that the `deny` and `allow` directives are in sequence, so it will deny the IP 192.168.1.1 while it allows the network 192.168.1.0/24 to access. A final `deny all;` directive makes sure that no other IP can access this location (`http://www.example1.com`).

So all other IPs, when they try to access this HTTP location, will get a 403 forbidden page. You can use the `error_page` directive to rewrite this to a 404 page.

There's more....

It is important to realize that the sequence of the directives is critical. Something like:

```
server {
listen 80;
server_name www.example1.com;
location / {
  deny all; # this is not a good idea
  deny     192.168.1.1;
  allow    192.168.1.0/24;
}
...
}
```

Will give a 403 forbidden to all the clients that open the location (`http://www.example1.com`).

Setting up simple rate limiting for a download directory

We have looked at ways to rate limit requests, but sometimes the issue is that some clients start to hog the bandwidth and pull down the quality of service for the other users. In such scenarios, it is best to use bandwidth based rate limiting.

The best application of something like this is with the static files on your site. It ensures that no one leeches your bandwidth for the wrong reasons.

How to do it...

The following simple configuration in the server directive will allow you to rate limit the whole site:

```
server {
server_name www.example1.com;
location /downloads/ {
    limit_rate  10k;
    root /var/www/www.example1.com/downloads/;
}
..
}
```

How it works...

This simple configuration will limit the /downloads file downloading speed to 10k for all users.

There's more...

There are a lot more things that can be done with this rate limiting; the following configuration will let you limit the rate to 100k after the 1 megabyte of the file has been sent in full throttle to the client:

```
server {
server_name www.example1.com;
location /downloads/ {
limit_rate_after 1m;
limit_rate 100k;
    root /var/www/www.example1.com/downloads/;
}
...
}
```

Rate limiting search engine bots

Till now we have learned about easy ways of blocking, request-limiting, and bandwidth-limiting all clients. We can start applying most of this knowledge to some problems that do come up in the production environment.

Most of the time, it so happens that with content heavy sites, bots and search engines start using up more bandwidth than actual users. In such a scenario, where you want to make sure the actual users are not hindered, yet you have the SEO intact, you will want to rate limit search engine bots.

How to do it...

This following configuration, when placed within the location directive, will help you block and rate limit some bots:

```
if($http_user_agent ~ "Alexibot|Art-Online|asterias|BackDoorbot|Black.
Hole|\
BlackWidow|BlowFish|botALot|BuiltbotTough|Bullseye|BunnySlippers|Cegbf
eieh|Cheesebot") {
    deny all;
}
if ($http_user_agent ~ Google|Yahoo|MSN|baidu) {
    limit_rate 20k;
}
```

How it works...

The idea is fairly simple, in cases where it is clear that the bot is not getting you traffic but only leeching your bandwidth, it is best to block them. But not all bots are bad. Googlebot, yahoobot and msnbot are all crucial for your search engine traffic to come through. It is a fine balance that has to be undertaken in situations where you have a high traffic site.

There's more....

You can use this situation to also ensure that your site gets very little spam traffic. It is clear that most commenting bots can be stopped with simple blacklisting of the HTTP_REFERER, as shown in the following snippet:

```
if ($http_referer ~* (\.us$|dating|diamond|forsale|girl|jewelry|organi
c|poker|poweroversoftware|teen|webcam|zippo) ) {
    deny all;
}
```

Setting up GeoIP using the MaxMind country database

MaxMind is a company that specializes in generating databases which map countries and cities to IP ranges. It allows you to easily locate the geographic location of the end client. This information can be used to show the user geo-dependent data, or maybe redirect to server locations that can serve the end-client faster.

In this recipe, we will install the MaxMind database in Nginx and show the usage of the GeoIP variables inside the Nginx configuration. Check out their demo at: `http://www.maxmind.com/app/locate_my_ip`.

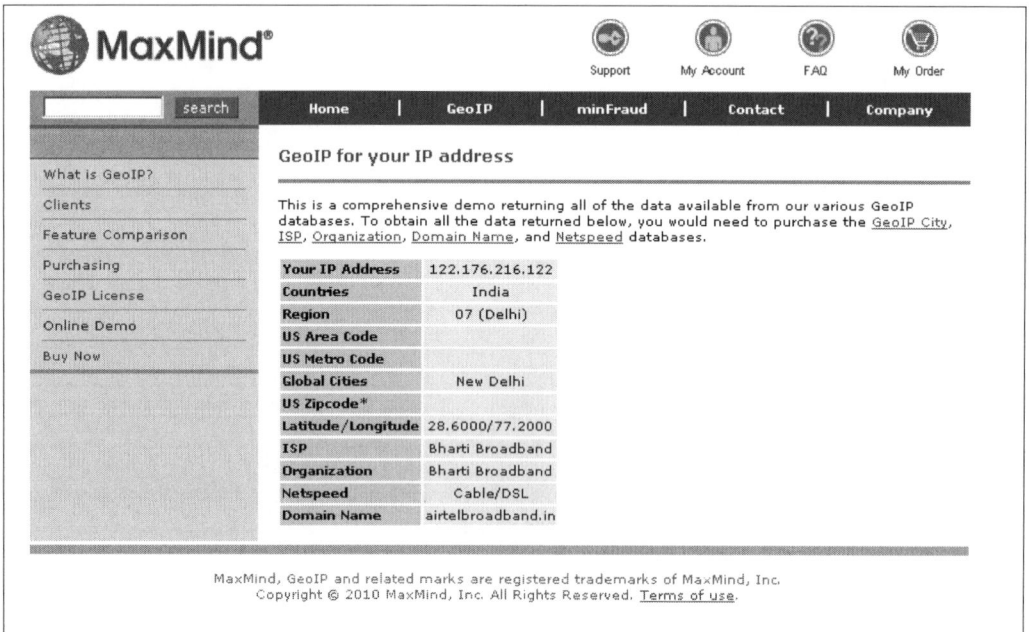

How to do it...

1. Download the Geo-IP database or install the package:

    ```
    wget http://geolite.maxmind.com/download/geoip/database/
    GeoLiteCity.dat.gz
    ```

    or

    ```
    aptitude install geoip-database
    ```

2. You will need to install some GeoIP libraries:

```
aptitude install libgeoip-dev
```

3. Then you configure Nginx for installing the GeoIP module as well. This assumes that you have already downloaded the Nginx codebase and have the compilation dependencies already installed. This has been covered in one of the earlier recipes as well.

```
./configure --with-http_geoip_module
```

4. We will then add the following configuration user the http directive:

```
http {
    geoip_country  GeoIP.dat; # the country IP database
    geoip_city     GeoLiteCity.dat; # the city IP database
    . . .
```

How it works...

The preceding steps installs the databases and configures the GeoIP module in Nginx. This allows the configuration to access the following new variables. These variables can let you write geography specific rules!

Variable	Purpose
$geoip_city_country_code	Two-letter country code, for example, "RU", "US".
$geoip_city_country_code3	Three-letter country code, for example, "RUS", "USA".
$geoip_city_country_name	The name of the country, for example, "Russian Federation", "United States" — if available.
$geoip_region	The name of the region (province, region, state, province, federal land, and the like), for example, "Moscow City", "DC" — if available.
$geoip_city	The name of the city, for example, "Moscow", "Washington", "Lisbon", &c — if available.
$geoip_postal_code	Zip code or postal code — if available.
$geoip_city_continent_code	Continent – if available
$geoip_latitude	Latitude — if available.
$geoip_longitude	Longitude — if available.

Using the GeoIP module to set up access and rate control

Now we come to an interesting part of Nginx, where we can use the GeoIP module to set up access and rate control.

For example, you can make your site inaccessible to a whole country depending on your needs. Hulu videos (`http://www.hulu.com`) are not available to IPs outside of the United States. This is, of course, not completely fool-proof as there are anonymity networks that allow you to mask your actual IP or appear as if you are a client from the US.

How to do it...

This simple configuration, which assumes that you have already installed GeoIP as per the preceding recipe, will allow Bermuda users to access certain content while blocking Bhutan and Bolivia users from accessing the site:

```
http {
    geoip_country  GeoIP.dat; # the country IP database
    geoip_city     GeoLiteCity.dat; # the city IP database
...
server {
server_name www.example1.com;
        ...
        location / {
        If($geoip_city_country_code ~ BM) {
        rate_limit 20k;
        }
        If($geoip_city_country_code ~ BT|BO) {
        deny all;
        }
          ...
}
...
}
```

How it works...

The idea behind the GeoIP module is simple. It basically looks at the remote client IP and fills up some variables which let you easily identify the various geographic attributes of the client. In this example, we are filtering requests that are from the Bermudas and rate limiting their bandwidth to 20k, while we are taking requests that are identified as coming from Bhutan and sending a 403 forbidden response to them.

You can extend this to create alternate sites for different countries on the same URL. This is useful for language localization as well. Nginx is clearly state-of-the-art when it comes to GeoIP mapping.

5
Let's be Secure: Security Modules

In this chapter, we will cover:

- ▸ Setting up HTTP auth for access control
- ▸ Generating a secure link for files
- ▸ Setting up HTTPS for a simple site
- ▸ Using non standard error codes for debugging SSL setup
- ▸ Using wildcard certificates with multiple servers
- ▸ Using Nginx SSL variables for rewrite rules

Introduction

Internet security has become one of the hottest topics of research and progress in recent time. Most countries have government mandates to run cyber-security teams in conjunction with normal security forces. Nginx, due to its rather small footprint and clear modular design, has a distinct advantage in maintaining a secure codebase in comparison to lots of much larger open source web servers.

It is fair to say that there is no web server with zero exploits; the only way to prevent security issues is to have the right policy in place. A policy is inclusive of the activities that others in the system can perform and the various security logging mechanisms in place. However, all policies are only as good as the implementation through correct configuration. A simple example is that we can use simple HTTP authentication to prevent random people from accessing a staging site. Here, the policy is to prevent unknown individuals from accessing your private beta site.

In this chapter we will look at how we can use the security modules built-in Nginx to secure your site and user's data.

Setting up HTTP auth for access control

In recent APIs, some of the larger web properties have utilized HTTP auth as a way of access control for their APIs. This however, has been gradually phased out for OAuth based authentication in most applications. The advantage of this scheme is that it's fairly fast to implement and ship out as an API provider as it is based on HTTP headers. In this particular recipe we will set up HTTP auth on a particular end-point and test it out.

How to do it...

1. You will first need to create the `htpasswd` file using Apache utils. This file basically contains the username and password hash pairs, which are used to authenticate the users:

   ```
   htpasswd -c /etc/nginx/user_auth dipankar
   ```

   The preceding command will create a user `dipankar` and ask for a password from the command line.

2. Now we basically add this configuration to the location portion of the configuration, where we want to protect the URL end-point using HTTP authentication:

   ```
   server {
   server_name www.example1.com;

   . . .

   location  /  {
     auth_basic           "Restricted";
     auth_basic_user_file  /etc/nginx/user_auth;
     . . .
   }
   }
   ```

3. Now you can go to `http://www.example1.com` and test the HTTP authentication. If you enter `dipankar` and the password that you used earlier, you will be successfully able to enter, as shown in the following screenshot:

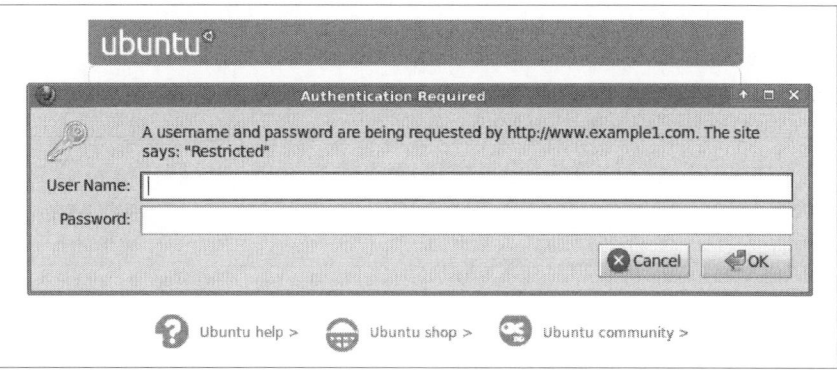

If you are unable to enter the correct combination of username and password you will get the "Authorization Required" page as in the following screenshot:

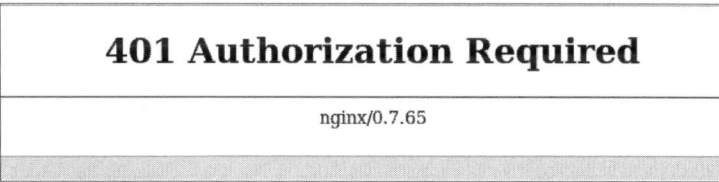

How it works...

The above configuration needs an authentication file which contains the list of users and passwords in the traditional Apache `htpasswd` format, and you can use it to password-protect any part of the site that you want to.

It is just as easy to have a different set of username passwords for password protecting other URLs on the site; you just need to create a separate set of `htpasswd` files.

Generating a secure link for files

Sometimes the only form of security that one needs for sharing files is a special URL. This is useful when the data is online temporarily, or maybe has value for a limited period of time. Nginx provides a module for exactly that purpose as well. In this recipe we will look at how to quickly implement secure links for files on your web server.

How to do it...

1. The first step is to ensure that Nginx is compiled with this module, so you will need to make sure that you download Nginx and use the following flag during compilation:

```
./configure . . . --with-http_secure_link_module
```

2. The next step is to choose a secret key (for example, `superhash`) and then use the following configuration:

```
location /t/ {
    secure_link_secret superhash;

    # If the hash is incorrect then $secure_link has the value of
      the null string.
    if ($secure_link = "") {
        return 403;
    }

    # This needs to be here otherwise you'll get a 404.
    rewrite ^ /t/$secure_link break;
}
```

3. Now we can test this on a file (`top_secret.html`) that we have, so the generated URL is of the form `http://www.example1.com/t/<md5 hash>/top_secret.html` where

```
echo -n 'top_secret.htmlsuperhash' | openssl dgst -md5
```

generates the `<md5 hash>`

4. If the above generated hash is correct, then you will be able to download the file. Otherwise, you will go to an Error page:

If you by mistake you enter the wrong hash, you will receive a "Forbidden" page as shown in the following screenshot:

How it works...

The idea is to create a simple mechanism to have a unique and difficult URL to generate for a given file. In this case, the combination of the filename and the secret salt is used to generate the MD5 hash to form a part of the URL.

Setting up HTTPS for a simple site

Cryptography has evolved over the ages and in today's world public key cryptography is pretty much the cutting edge (this is what PGP is based upon). All browsers implement certificate based security, allowing for safe and encrypted transactions on the Internet. It has proven to be one of the key factors contributing to the growth of e-commerce over the last decade.

Just as most browsers implement SSL based client mechanisms, all web servers also need to handle the server end of things. Nginx has a very clean and easy-to-configure implementation of SSL-based security. In this recipe we will have a look at how easy it is to get a pair of certificates and quickly set up a secure site.

How to do it...

1. Initially, you will need to buy a certificate from one of the known Certificate Authority (CAs) or obtain it from a free, public CA such as CAcert. Alternatively you can generate a certificate yourself. You can read more about this by picking up a Packt publications book on server security. These certificates basically come with 2 files, one of which is the certificate and the other a key. Let's say they are called `cert.pem` and `cert.key`. They are always specific to the domain that you are using it for.

2. To implement SSL on a certain end-point you will need to make sure that your firewall has the right ports open (80,443).

3. The following piece of configuration has to be placed in the configuration file for the particular domain (in this case `www.example1.com`).

```
server {
 server_name www.example1.com;
  listen 443 default ssl;
  ssl_certificate       /usr/local/nginx/conf/cert.pem;
  ssl_certificate_key   /usr/local/nginx/conf/cert.key;

 . . .

}
```

4. Now you can just try out `https://www.example1.com`, and it should open without any errors. If there are errors, it implies that the certificates are not being validated correctly by the browser. In the following example we can see how Paypal (`https://www.paypal.com`) has a valid certificate from Verisign Inc:

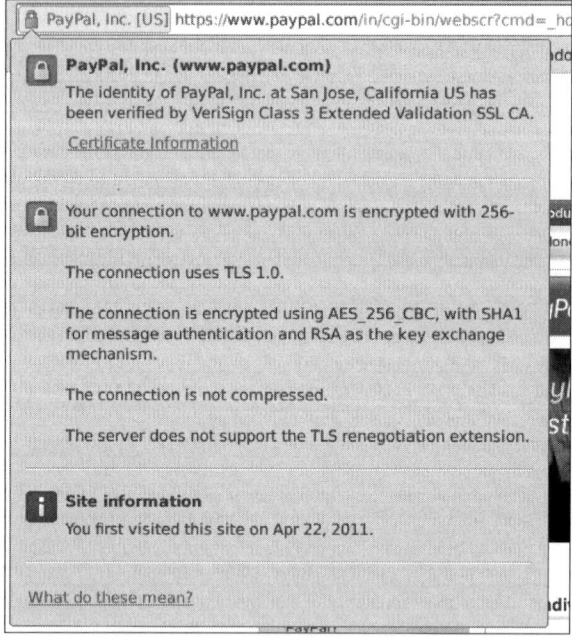

In a lot of cases, the certificate of the site may not be correctly configured, or may have expired. In those cases, most modern browsers will ask the user if they want to navigate to such a site, as shown in the following screenshot. It is advised, in most cases, to remove badly configured certificates as they may act as a barrier for the end user.

How it works...

The following image best describes the actual process of SSL authentication. In the configuration, we basically define the certificate and the key for the web server, and the rest is pretty much handled internally:

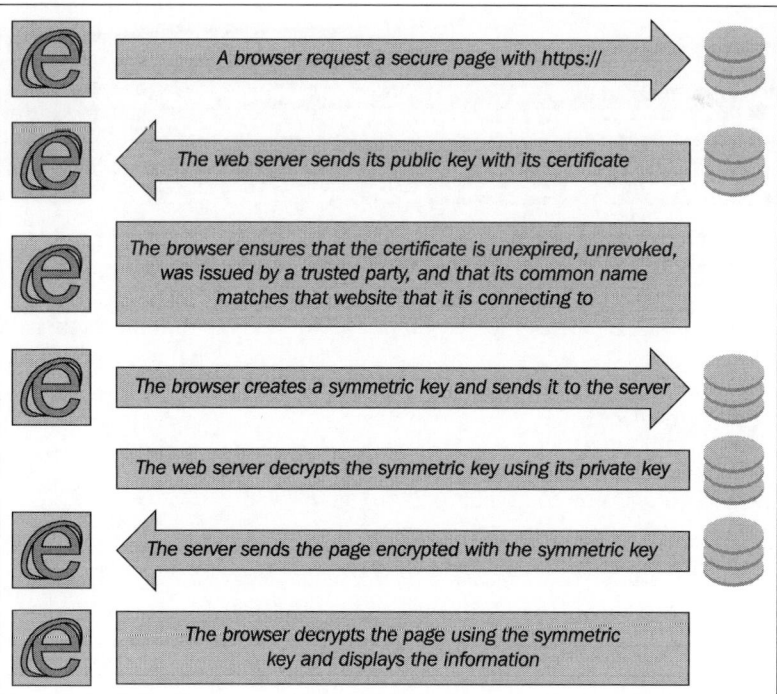

There's more...

Let's say that you do not yet want to buy certificates for your site, and want instead to try out SSL based security for you site. You can generate your certificates by following the steps below:

1. First, change directory to where you want to create the certificate and private key, for example:

    ```
    cd /usr/local/nginx/conf
    ```

2. Now create the server private key. You'll be asked for a passphrase:

    ```
    openssl genrsa -des3 -out server.key 1024
    ```

3. Create the Certificate Signing Request (CSR):

    ```
    openssl req -new -key server.key -out server.csr
    ```

4. Remove the necessity of entering a passphrase for starting up Nginx with SSL using the above private key:

    ```
    cp server.key server.key.org

    openssl rsa -in server.key.org -out server.key
    ```

5. Finally, sign the certificate using the above private key and CSR:

    ```
    openssl x509 -req -days 365 -in server.csr -signkey server.key
    -out server.crt
    ```

Using non standard error codes for debugging SSL setup

Most setups are difficult to get the first time around, and to that end Nginx has provided some really easy-to-use non-standard error codes for debugging your SSL setup.

In this recipe we will take a look at the non-standard error codes that are present and how to tackle SSL setup issues.

How to do it...

These error codes are enabled by default and are as follows:

HTTP error codes	Error
495	Error checking client certificate
496	Client did not grant the required certificate
497	Normal request was sent to HTTPS

How it works...

The idea is fairly simple. Nginx allows you to log these special errors that you can use to identify and correct SSL issues.

A simple example is that you can create a simple page that looks at all the Nginx variables on a particular error code for debugging purposes only. If you get a 495 error page it implies that the client certificate was not successfully checked from the CA it was issued from. This may be for reasons such as firewall permissions or the fact that you may have resolution issues on the web server. In some situations, when you get 496 it may indicate that someone is attempting to create some issues with your site! Most SSL attacks involve a man-in-the middle scenario or replay attacks where there is a small proxy server that sits in the middle and records all the above steps necessary to create a SSL connection, only to target and cause havoc at a later time.

Using wildcard certificates with multiple servers

In lots of situations, we would want to provide a lot of secured subdomains among unsecured ones and share resources, both across the HTTP and HTTPS subdomains. In this recipe we will have a look at how to configure a HTTP domain, a secured subdomain and a directory shared on both HTTP and HTTPS subdomains.

How to do it...

To achieve the above, all we need to do is to add the following to the configuration. It assumes that all the certificate files have been concatenated into one file (common.crt) and similarly all the keys have been concatenated as well (common.key):

```
http{
    ...
    ssl_certificate        common.crt;
    ssl_certificate_key    common.key;
    server {
        listen          80;
        server_name     www.example1.com;
        location / {
            ...
        }
    }
    server {
        listen          443 default ssl;
```

```
            server_name      payment.example1.com;
            location / {
            ...
            }
        }
        server {
          listen          80;
          listen          443;
          server_name     static.example1.com;
          location / {
                root /var/www/www.example1.com/static;
          }
        }
```

Now if you visit the three different parts of the site, you will realize that you can access `http://www.example1.com` and `http://static.example1.com/null.gif` but not be able to access `https://www.example1.com` or `http://payment.example1.com/`. The following screenshot demonstrates `https://www.example1.com` not opening:

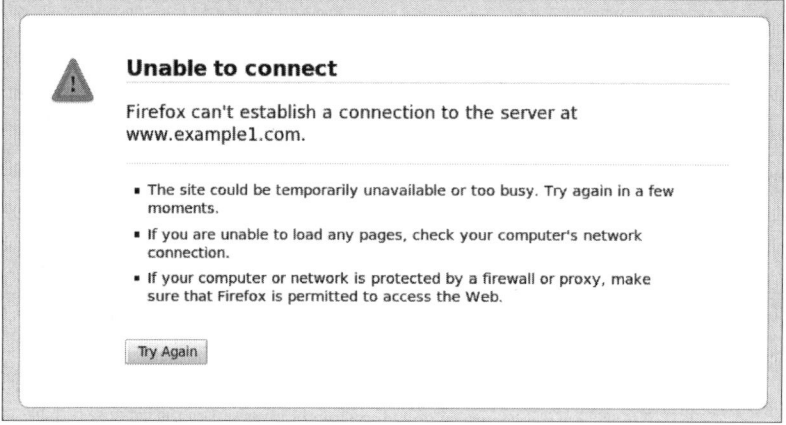

The following screenshot displays the `null.gif` file being served correctly by Nginx, while `https://www.example1.com` does not open as shown in the preceding screenshot.

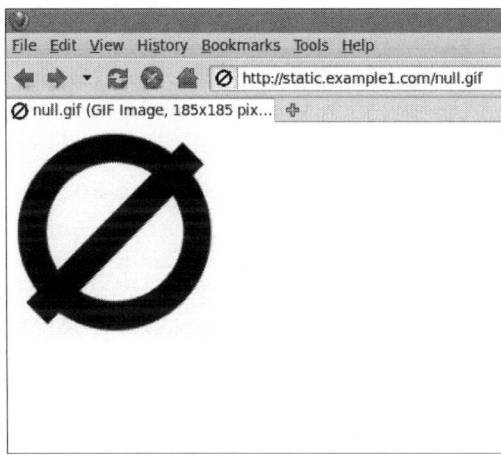

How it works...

This particular configuration shows the versatility of Nginx. In this recipe, you simply turned SSL on and off depending on the domain. You had one case where you did not want SSL (`http://www.example1.com`), another in which you wanted only SSL (`https://payment.example1.com`), and a third case where both the SSL and non-SSL URLs were enabled for the files in a particular directory (`/var/www/www.example1.com/static`).

Using Nginx SSL variables for rewrite rules

Nginx has a very smart and well-designed rewrite system. It even allows you to access SSL variables for your rewrite rules. In this recipe, we will explore a simple example to see what we can do with these variables. You can explore more about rewrite rules in _Chapter 2_ which focuses on rewrites.

We will basically check if the SSL verification (`$ssl_client_verify`) was a success and show a different set of pages if it was not.

How to do it...

Inserting this configuration in your file will basically result in showing the user a different site if the SSL client certificate is successfully verified:

```
server {
  listen          ssl;
  server_name     www.example1.com;
  if($ssl_client_verify ~* SUCCESS) {
     rewrite ^ http://www.example1.com/test/;
```

```
        }
        location / {
        ...
        }
        location /test/ {
        }
    }
```

How it works...

This simple example has a look at how we caused the client certificate validation to redirect the client to a different part of the site (in this case `http://www.example1.com/test/`).

You can use other variables that the SSL module populates for a given session to do other things, like protocol based logging and more.

There's more...

You can access the following variables that can be utilized in creating interesting rules:

SSL variable	Description
`$ssl_cipher`	This returns the cipher suite being used for the currently established SSL/TLS connection.
`$ssl_client_serial`	This returns the serial number of the client certificate for the currently established SSL/TLS connection, if applicable. That is, if client authentication is activated in the connection.
`$ssl_client_s_dn`	This returns the subject Distinguished Name (DN) of the client certificate for the currently established SSL/TLS connection, if applicable. That is, if client authentication is activated in the connection.
`$ssl_client_i_dn`	This returns the issuer DN of the client certificate for the currently established SSL/TLS connection, if applicable. That is, if client authentication is activated in the connection.
`$ssl_protocol`	This returns the protocol of the currently established SSL/TLS connection, depending on the configuration and client available options, it's one of SSLv2, SSLv3, or TLSv1.
`$ssl_session_id`	The Session ID of the established secure connection—requires Nginx version greater or equal to 0.8.20.
`$ssl_client_cert`	Returns the client certificate installed for the particular domain.
`$ssl_client_raw_cert`	Returns the raw client certificate.
`$ssl_client_verify`	Takes the value "SUCCESS" when the client certificate is successfully verified.

6
Setting Up Applications: FCGI and WSGI Modules

In this chapter, we will cover:

- ▶ Setting up a PHP FCGI site
- ▶ Setting up a Python site using uWSGI
- ▶ Modifying FCGI timeouts
- ▶ Utilizing FCGI cache to speed it up
- ▶ Using multiple FCGI backends

Introduction

This is a practical section devoted to helping programmers and system administrators to understand and install their applications using Nginx as the web server. Due to the lack of integrated modules for running PHP and Python, the setting up of such systems can be an issue for non-experienced system administrators.

Nginx is designed to be a framework to handle native web and mail protocols using an event driven mechanism. Most of the web server-application interfaces have been added to the main web server later. Over time, CGI has evolved into many forms. It has resulted FCGI, SCGI, and similar protocol WSGI for python. The goal at the end of the day for all these protocols is to effectively communicate with the web server in a standardized format with the lowest possible language overheads.

Setting up a PHP FCGI site

This recipe helps you to set up a PHP site using Nginx and PHP-fpm fairly easily and quickly. Nginx, unlike Apache, does not have mod_php built into it and remains a standalone web server which supports many standard protocols such as CGI, FCGI, SCGI, WSGI, and more through core and third-party modules.

PHP-fpm is a set of utilities and scripts that enables the system administrator to easily run and manage a PHP FCGI backend. This is officially available as a part of the PHP5.3.x stable and would become a major part of PHP deployment going forward.

We will initially have a look at how to set up php-fpm and then see a simple WordPress site being configured using this setup.

How to do it...

This will be divided into two sections; one which will help you install php-fpm and the other which will help you configure WordPress on Nginx using this setup.

Installing php-fpm for PHP 5.2.x

1. Depending on your system and PHP requirements you will need to either download the packages [deb/rpm] or the source code.

2. If you are lucky, you can work with the packages you can download from http://php-fpm.org/download/ depending on the version of PHP that you have.

3. If you are not in luck for the packages, you will need to follow the guide on the following site: http://legacy.php-fpm.org/Documentation. In this guide you will effectively download the latest patch for PHP 5.2.X and then apply the patch:

    ```
    bzip2 -cd php-5.2.11.tar.bz2 | tar xf -
    patch -d php-5.2.11 -p1 <php-fpm-0.6~5.2.patch
    cd php-5.2.11
    ./buildconf --force
    ./configure --enable-fastcgi --with-fpm --with-libevent[=path]
    ```

4. After the installation is done, you can start the php-fpm daemon process. This will by default run on the 9000 port (or you can configure it according to your needs).

Configuring WordPress

1. Now we will simply create a new configuration for the WordPress site that you plan to run with Nginx and PHP-FPM. This assumes that the php-fpm is listening on port 9000.

```
server {
    listen        80;
    server_name   www.example1.com;
    root    /var/www/www.example1.com;
    index   index.php index.html index.htm;

    try_files $uri $uri/ /index.php;
    location ~ \.php$ {
        include fastcgi_params;
        fastcgi_pass    127.0.0.1:9000;
        fastcgi_index   index.php;
    }
}
```

2. Now all you need to do is restart Nginx and make sure that it accepts the configuration.

3. After this, we can access the domain that has been set up and that will redirect you to the installation page, as displayed in the following screenshot:

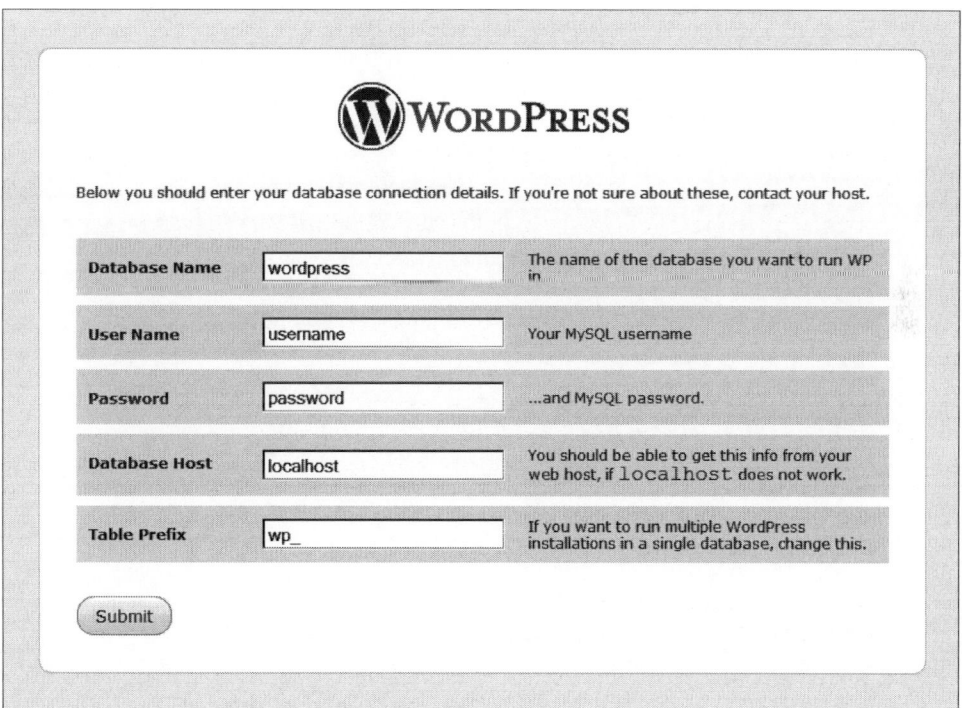

4. You will need to make sure that you have created a MySQL database on your system, as the next installation screen requires you to enter the database information:

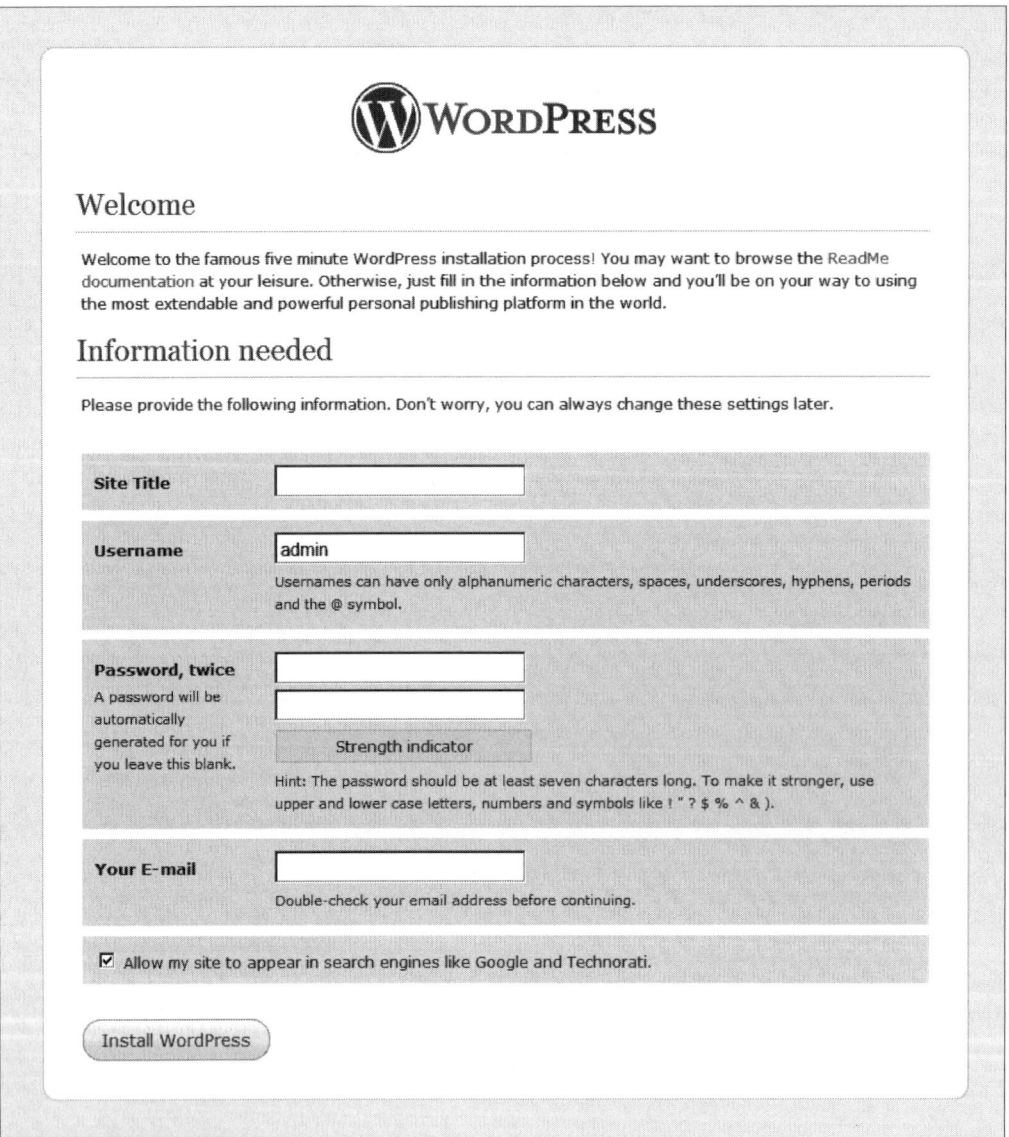

5. Finally, you will have got your PHP WordPress blog up and running!

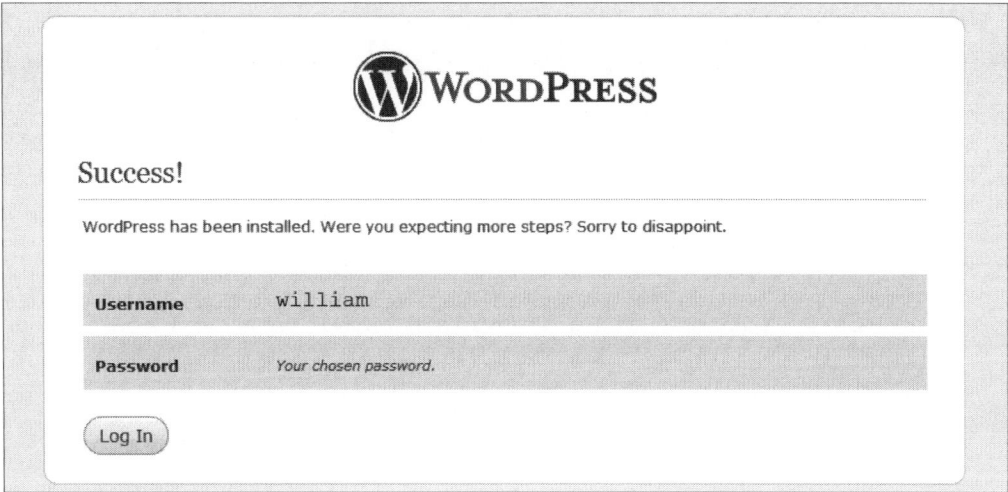

How it works...

Depending on the operating system and PHP version, you will have to choose the correct method of installing php-fpm. After the installation, you will need to start the php-fpm daemon installed on a port that is not already in use by any other application.

The Nginx configuration step involves setting up a server directive which will basically invoke the daemon with the HTTP request and the script being queried. We are also handling WordPress clean URLs using the above rewrites.

There's more...

You can also go ahead and install other PHP applications without any clean URLs by simply using the following sample configuration! In this case, we do not require any of the static files and clean URL rewrites.

```
server {
    listen        80;
    server_name   www.example1.com;
    root    /var/www/www.example1.com;
    index   index.php index.html index.htm;

    location ~ \.php$ {
        include fastcgi_conf;
        fastcgi_pass    127.0.0.1:9000;
        fastcgi_index   index.php;
    }
}
```

Setting up a Python site using uWSGI

Python has seen an immense rise of popularity ever since it was adopted by Google for a significant part of its server side scripting. It has garnered significant support from the industry and consequently warrants attention in this practical chapter.

There has been development of **Web Server Gateway Interface** (WSGI) which acts as a simple and universal interface between a web server and the various Python frameworks that have come up in recent times. In this recipe, we will use a sample installation of Django, which is a Python web framework, to show how we can get Nginx and python to work together.

How to do it...

For setting up a simple python, we will look at three parts. The first part will deal with the installation of uWSGI (`http://projects.unbit.it/uwsgi/wiki`), the second will deal with the setting up a very basic Django installation, and the last will deal with how to get them all working together.

Installation of uWSGI

1. If you are using a Nginx which is greater than 0.8.4 then uWSGI is already installed on your server. Otherwise you will need to follow the steps below. It is also assumed that you have root privileges or `sudo` access to the server on which the installation is to be done.

2. Download the uWSGI module at the same level of your Nginx source code directory and then configure the package:

   ```
   wget http://projects.unbit.it/downloads/uwsgi-0.9.6.5.tar.gz

   tar -xvzf  uwsgi-0.9.6.5.tar.gz

   cd nginx

   ./configure --add-module=../uwsgi-0.9.6.5/nginx/

   make && make install
   ```

3. This will install the uWSGI module for your Nginx setup. You will also need to copy the `uwsgi_params` file into your Nginx installation directory.

Basic Django setup with WSGI script

1. We will first install the easy_install script from `http://peak.telecommunity.com/dist/ez_setup.py`

   ```
   sudo python http://peak.telecommunity.com/dist/ez_setup.py
   ```

2. We will then install the Django package using `easy_install`, this will handle all the dependencies and install them for you.

   ```
   sudo easy_install django
   ```

3. After this, we will start a new project called `test`

```
django-admin.py startproject testapp
```

4. We can now test if it is running or not by simply going into the test directory and invoking the in-built development server:

```
cd test
```

```
python manage.py runserver
```

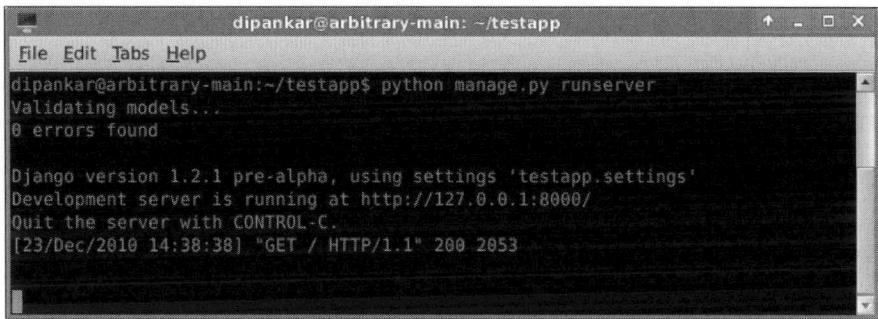

5. We will now create the WSGI file that will run this test setup. You will need to go above the test directory and create a new file called `django_wsgi.py`:

```
import os
os.environ['DJANGO_SETTINGS_MODULE'] = 'testapp.settings'

import django.core.handlers.wsgi

application = django.core.handlers.wsgi.WSGIHandler()
```

6. You will now need to run a uWSGI instance for this site using the following command. This assumes that the project was created at `/var/www/` and the port that uWSGI will use is 3031.

```
uwsgi --socket 127.0.0.1:3031 --pythonpath /var/www/ --pythonpath
/var/www/testapp/ -w django_wsgi -M -T -d server.log -L
```

Nginx with uWSGI

1. For running this test Django site, you will need to add the following configuration:

```
server {
    listen        80;
    server_name   www.example1.com;
    location / {
        root    /var/www/testapp;
        index   index.php index.html index.htm;
    }
    location / {
```

```
                    uwsgi_pass    127.0.0.1:3031;
                    include       uwsgi_params;
            }
       }
```

2. You will need to restart the Nginx web server and then you can try visiting your site.

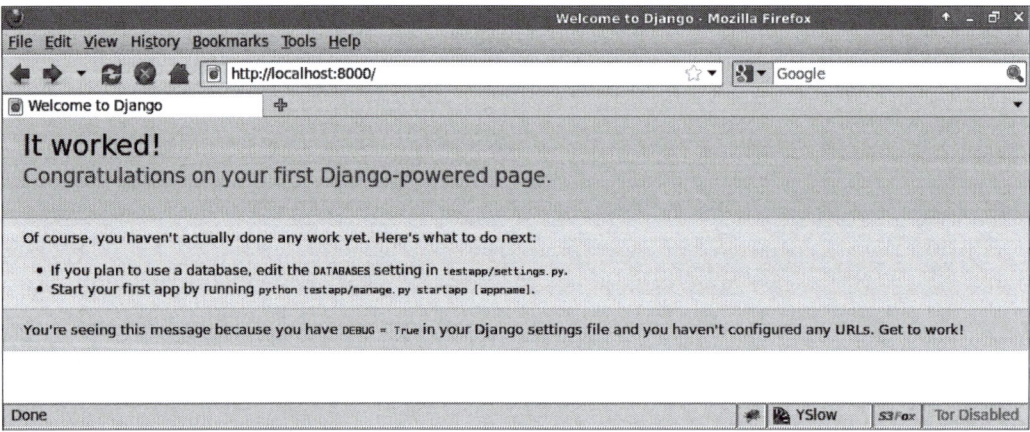

How it works...

The idea behind uWSGI is to provide a common protocol between the application and the web server so that you can plug and play depending on your needs. In this recipe, we can clearly see how one can go about uWSGI, which in some cases already comes as a part of the Nginx source package. We can see how to create and get a small Django application running.

So the uWSGI daemon runs on the 3031 port in our example and Nginx basically converts the HTTP requests into the WSGI protocol and proxies them to the daemon. uWSGI provides quite a lot of features which allow you to also manage the python overheads properly.

There's more...

You can take this simple example and extend it to most other python frameworks. Here is a really small standalone python script for web.py developers. Save this as django_usgi2.py:

```
import web
urls = (
    '/(.*)', 'hello'
)
app = web.application(urls, globals())
class hello:
    def GET(self, name):
```

```
        if not name:
            name = 'World'
        return 'Hello, ' + name + '!'
    application = app.wsgifunc()
```

To run this use:

```
uwsgi -s /tmp/web.py.socket -w django_usgi2.py
```

Modifying FCGI timeouts

If you have already discovered the various possibilities of how to set up PHP with Nginx, it will become clear that FCGI is a fairly optimal setup for low to medium traffic environments for PHP and Python, where RAM is a constraint.

In situations where due to resource constraints or time-consuming computation the FCGI daemon is not able to send back a response quickly enough, the user is made to wait and this lowers the quality of experience for the site.

How to do it...

In order to increase your FCGI timeout from the default 60 second you will need to add the following to your FCGI directives:

```
server {
    listen          80;
    server_name  www.example1.com;
    root    /var/www/www.example1.com;
    index  index.php index.html index.htm;
    fastcgi_read_timeout  120;
    fastcgi_write_timeout  120;

    try_files $uri $uri/ /index.php;
    location ~ \.php$ {
        include fastcgi_params;
        fastcgi_pass    127.0.0.1:9000;
        fastcgi_index  index.php;
    }
}
```

How it works...

These simple directives simply increase the amount of time the server waits for the upstream FCGI process to process and send data. This is important as other directives like send_ timeout and proxy_connect_timeout do not affect the Nginx FCGI upstream setting.

We are utilizing the same Nginx setup from the recipe use to set up PHP-fpm with Nginx in the above configuration.

Utilizing FCGI cache to speed it up

Due to the disconnected nature of the Nginx and the FCGI daemon, a cache in between can really speed things up for common requests. If set up correctly it can do wonders for a site and the server as the CPU will not be utilized unnecessarily.

How to do it...

It is pretty easy to setup:

```
http {
    fastcgi_cache_path    /var/www/cache   levels=1:2
                          keys_zone=NAME:10m
                          inactive=5m;
    server {
      server_name wwww.example1.com;
      ...
      location / {
        ...
        fastcgi_pass    127.0.0.1:9000;
        fastcgi_cache    NAME;
        fastcgi_cache_valid    200 302   1h;
        fastcgi_cache_valid    301       1d;
        fastcgi_cache_valid    any       1m;
        fastcgi_cache_min_uses  1;
        fastcgi_cache_use_stale error  timeout invalid_header http_500;
      }
    }
}
```

How it works...

In this recipe we are setting up a cache called `NAME` and setting it up for the site, with an hour of caching on any site that was successfully retrieved, while very low caching for error pages.

The `fastcgi_cache_path` directive specifies the path to the cache storage and other cache parameters. All data is stored within this directive, the cache key and the name of the cache file are calculated as the MD5 sum of the proxied URL. The levels parameter sets the number and width of the name of the sub directories to be used in the caching file location. The size has been set to 10M in the current example, and by default, entries are removed from the chache if inactive for ten minutes.

The following table summarizes the various directives and their use:

Directive	Use
fastcgi_cache	This determines the area which will be utilized for caching
fastcgi_cache_key	This sets the key that will be used for caching
fastcgi_cache_path	This sets the path and other critical parameters for the cache being created
fastcgi_cache_methods	This sets which HTTP methods are to be allowed while caching
fastcgi_cache_min_uses	This specifies how many requests to the same URL will be cached
fastcgi_cache_use_stale	This determines if the web server will start serving stale cached data in case of gateway errors
fastcgi_cache_valid	This sets the caching period for the specified HTTP codes

Using multiple FCGI backends

In this recipe, we will look at how to work with multiple FCGI backends on the system. This can happen in a system where you have multiple types of applications running, such as a PHP application, a Python FCGI application, and so on.

It can also be the case that you want to isolate two application backends to prevent performance issues between them, as one slow application would definitely tie the other one down.

How to do it...

This is fairly straightforward, as you can create a simple `fcgi_common` file that will contain the common FCGI configuration:

```
fastcgi_param   SCRIPT_FILENAME   /var/www/www.example1.com$fastcgi_
script_name;

fastcgi_param   QUERY_STRING      $query_string;
fastcgi_param   REQUEST_METHOD    $request_method;
fastcgi_param   CONTENT_TYPE      $content_type;
fastcgi_param   CONTENT_LENGTH    $content_length;

fastcgi_param   SCRIPT_NAME       $fastcgi_script_name;
fastcgi_param   REQUEST_URI       $request_uri;
fastcgi_param   DOCUMENT_URI      $document_uri;
fastcgi_param   DOCUMENT_ROOT     $document_root;
fastcgi_param   SERVER_PROTOCOL   $server_protocol;

fastcgi_param   GATEWAY_INTERFACE CGI/1.1;
fastcgi_param   SERVER_SOFTWARE   nginx/$nginx_version;

fastcgi_param   REMOTE_ADDR       $remote_addr;
```

```
fastcgi_param    REMOTE_PORT          $remote_port;
fastcgi_param    SERVER_ADDR          $server_addr;
fastcgi_param    SERVER_PORT          $server_port;
fastcgi_param    SERVER_NAME          $server_name;

fastcgi_param    REDIRECT_STATUS      200;
```

You will then need to use the following configuration and put it in the Nginx configuration file at `sites-enabled/www.example1.com`:

```
server {
    listen        80;
    server_name   www.example1.com;

    location / {
        root     /var/www/www.example1.com;
        index    index.php index.html index.htm;
    }

    location ~ \.php$ {
        include fcgi_common;
fastcgi_pass    127.0.0.1:9000;
        fastcgi_index   index.php;
    }
}
```

You will then need to use the following configuration and put it in the Nginx configuration file at `sites-enabled/www.example2.com`

```
server {
    listen        80;
    server_name   www.example2.com;

    location / {
        root     /var/www/www.example2.com;
        index    index.php index.html index.htm;
    }

    location ~ \.php$ {
        include fcgi_common;
        fastcgi_pass    127.0.0.1:9001;
        fastcgi_index   index.php;
    }
}
```

How it works...

This setup basically lets you take out the common parts of the FCGI directives and have a clean setup for as many sites as you want.

If you notice, with this setup the rewrites specific for the clean URLs of an application are the only extra directives that are required.

7
Nginx as a Reverse Proxy

In this chapter, we will cover:

- ▶ Using Nginx as a simple reverse proxy
- ▶ Setting up a rails site using Nginx as a reverse proxy
- ▶ Setting up correct reverse proxy timeouts
- ▶ Setting up caching on the reverse proxy
- ▶ Using multiple backends for the reverse proxy
- ▶ Serving CGI files using thttpd and Nginx
- ▶ Setting up load balancing with reverse proxy
- ▶ Splitting requests based on various conditions using split-clients

Introduction

Nginx has found most applications acting as a reverse proxy for many sites. A reverse proxy is a type of proxy server that retrieves resources for a client from one or more servers. These resources are returned to the client as though they originated from the proxy server itself.

Due to its event driven architecture and C codebase, it consumes significantly lower CPU power and memory than many other better known solutions out there. This chapter will deal with the usage of Nginx as a reverse proxy in various common scenarios. We will have a look at how we can set up a rail application, set up load balancing, and also look at a caching setup using Nginx, which will potentially enhance the performance of your existing site without any codebase changes.

Using Nginx as a simple reverse proxy

Nginx in its simplest form can be used as a reverse proxy for any site; it acts as an intermediary layer for security, load distribution, caching, and compression purposes. In effect, it can potentially enhance the overall quality of the site for the end user without any change of application source code by distributing the load from incoming requests to multiple backend servers, and also caching static, as well as dynamic content.

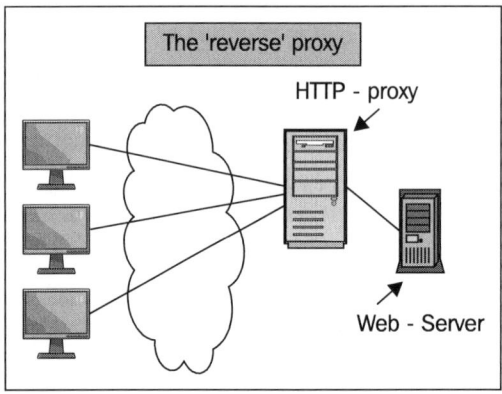

How to do it...

You will need to first define `proxy.conf`, which will be later included in the main configuration of the reverse proxy that we are setting up:

```
proxy_redirect          off;
proxy_set_header        Host            $host;
proxy_set_header        X-Real-IP       $remote_addr;
proxy_set_header        X-Forwarded-For $proxy_add_x_forwarded_for;
client_max_body_size    10m;
client_body_buffer_size 128k;
proxy_connect_timeout   90;
proxy_send_timeout      90;
proxy_read_timeout      90;s
proxy_buffers           32 4k
```

To use Nginx as a reverse proxy for a site running on a local port of the server, the following configuration will suffice:

```
server {
  listen    80;
  server_name   example1.com;
  access_log  /var/www/example1.com/log/nginx.access.log;
```

```
    error_log   /var/www/example1.com/log/nginx_error.log debug;
location / {
  include proxy.conf;
  proxy_pass           http://127.0.0.1:8080;
  }
}
```

How it works...

In this recipe, Nginx simply acts as a proxy for the defined backend server which is running on the 8080 port of the server, which can be any HTTP web application. Later in this chapter, other advanced recipes will have a look at how one can define more backend servers, and how we can set them up to respond to requests.

Setting up a rails site using Nginx as a reverse proxy

In this recipe, we will set up a working rails site and set up Nginx working on top of the application. This will assume that the reader has some knowledge of rails and thin. There are other ways of running Nginx and rails, as well, like using Passenger Phusion.

How to do it...

This will require you to set up thin first, then to configure thin for your application, and then to configure Nginx.

1. If you already have gems installed then the following command will install thin, otherwise you will need to install it from source:

   ```
   sudo gem install thin
   ```

2. Now you need to generate the thin configuration. This will create a configuration in the `/etc/thin` directory:

```
sudo thin config -C /etc/thin/myapp.yml -c /var/rails/myapp
--servers 5 -e production
```

3. Now you can start the thin service. Depending on your operating system the start up command will vary.

4. Assuming that you have Nginx installed, you will need to add the following to the configuration file:

```
upstream thin_cluster {
    server unix:/tmp/thin.0.sock;
    server unix:/tmp/thin.1.sock;
    server unix:/tmp/thin.2.sock;
    server unix:/tmp/thin.3.sock;
    server unix:/tmp/thin.4.sock;
}

server {
  listen       80;
  server_name  www.example1.com;

  root /var/www.example1.com/public;

  location / {
    proxy_set_header  X-Real-IP  $remote_addr;
    proxy_set_header  X-Forwarded-For $proxy_add_x_forwarded_for;
    proxy_set_header Host $http_host;
    proxy_redirect false;

    try_files $uri $uri/index.html $uri.html @thin;
    location @thin {
      include proxy.conf;
      proxy_pass http://thin_cluster;
    }
  }

  error_page   500 502 503 504   /50x.html;
  location = /50x.html {
    root    html;
  }
}
```

How it works...

This is a fairly simple rails stack, where we basically configure and run five upstream thin threads which interact with Nginx through socket connections.

There are a few rewrites that ensure that Nginx serves the static files, and all dynamic requests are processed by the rails backend. It can also be seen how we set proxy headers correctly to ensure that the client IP is forwarded correctly to the rails application. It is important for a lot of applications to be able to access the client IP to show geo-located information, and logging this IP can be useful in identifying if geography is a problem when the site is not working properly for specific clients.

Setting up correct reverse proxy timeouts

In this section we will set up correct reverse proxy timeouts which will affect your user's interaction when your backend application is unable to respond to the client's request.

In such a case, it is advisable to set up some sensible timeout pages so that the user can understand that further refreshing may only aggravate the issues on the web application.

How to do it...

You will first need to set up `proxy.conf` which will later be included in the configuration:

```
proxy_redirect            off;
proxy_set_header          Host              $host;
proxy_set_header          X-Real-IP         $remote_addr;
proxy_set_header          X-Forwarded-For $proxy_add_x_forwarded_for;
client_max_body_size      10m;
client_body_buffer_size   128k;
proxy_connect_timeout     90;
proxy_send_timeout        90;
proxy_read_timeout        90;s
proxy_buffers             32 4k
```

Reverse proxy timeouts are some fairly simple flags that we need to set up in the Nginx configuration like in the following example:

```
server {
  listen    80;
  server_name   example1.com;
  access_log   /var/www/example1.com/log/nginx.access.log;
  error_log   /var/www/example1.com/log/nginx_error.log debug;

  #set your default location
```

```
location / {
  include proxy.conf;
  proxy_read_timeout 120;
  proxy_connect_timeout 120;
  proxy_pass          http://127.0.0.1:8080;
 }
}
```

How it works...

In the preceding configuration we have set the following variables, it is fairly clear what these variables achieve in the context of the configurations:

Directive	Use
proxy_read_timeout	This directive sets the read timeout for the response of the proxied server. It determines how long Nginx will wait to get the response to a request. The timeout is established not for the entire response, but only between two operations of reading.
proxy_connect_timeout	This directive assigns timeout with the transfer of request to the upstream server. Timeout is established not on the entire transfer of request, but only between two write operations. If after this time the upstream server does not take new data, then Nginx shuts down the connection.

Setting up caching on the reverse proxy

In a setup where Nginx acts as the layer between the client and the backend web application, it is clear that caching can be one of the benefits that can be achieved. In this recipe, we will have a look at setting up caching for any site to which Nginx is acting as a reverse proxy. Due to extremely small footprint and modular architecture, Nginx has become quite the Swiss knife of the modern web stack.

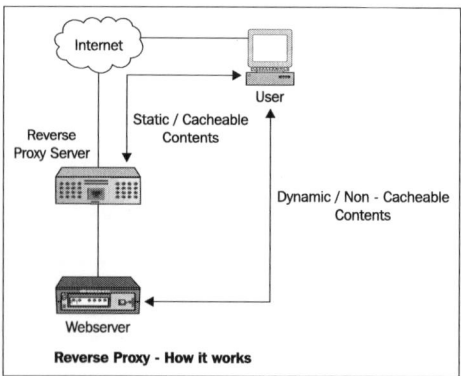

Reverse Proxy - How it works

How to do it...

This example configuration shows how we can use caching when utilizing Nginx as a reverse proxy web server:

```
http {
  proxy_cache_path  /var/www/cache levels=1:2 keys_zone=my-cache:8m
max_size=1000m inactive=600m;
  proxy_temp_path /var/www/cache/tmp;

...

server {
 listen    80;
 server_name   example1.com;
 access_log   /var/www/example1.com/log/nginx.access.log;
 error_log   /var/www/example1.com/log/nginx_error.log debug;
 #set your default location
 location / {
      include proxy.conf;
      proxy_pass          http://127.0.0.1:8080/;
      proxy_cache my-cache;
      proxy_cache_valid  200 302   60m;
      proxy_cache_valid  404       1m;

 }
}
}
```

How it works...

This configuration implements a simple cache with 1000MB maximum size, and keeps all HTTP response 200 pages in the cache for 60 minutes and HTTP response 404 pages in cache for 1 minute.

There is an initial directive that creates the cache file on initialization, in further directives we basically configure the location that is going to be cached.

 It is possible to actually set up more than one cache path for multiple locations.

There's more...

This was a relatively small show of what can be achieved with the caching aspect of the proxy module. Here are some more directives that can be really useful in optimizing and making your stack faster and more efficient:

Directive	Use
proxy_cache_bypass	The directive specifies the conditions under which the answer will not be taken from the cache. If one string variable is not empty and not equal to "0", the answer is not taken from the cache.
proxy_cache_min_uses	This directive determines the number of accesses before a page is cached.
proxy_cache_use_stale	This directive tells Nginx when to serve a stale item from the proxy cache. For example, when an Application error HTTP Code 500 occurs.
proxy_cache_methods	This directive lets you choose what directives to cache [GET, PUT, and so on].

Using multiple backends for the reverse proxy

As traffic increases, the need to scale the site up becomes a necessity. With a transparent reverse proxy like Nginx in front, most users never even see the scaling affecting their interactions with the site. Usually, for smaller sites one backend process is sufficient to handle the oncoming traffic. As the site popularity increases, the first solution is to increase the number of backend processes and let Nginx multiplex the client requests. This recipe takes a look at how to add new backend processes to Nginx.

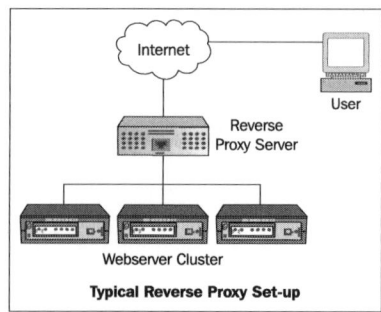

Typical Reverse Proxy Set-up

How to do it...

The configuration below adds three upstream servers to which client requests will be sent for processing:

```
upstream backend  {
  server backend1.example1.com weight=5;
  server backend2.example1.com max_fails=3  fail_timeout=30s;
  server backend3.example1.com;
}
server {
 listen    80;
 server_name   example1.com;
 access_log   /var/www/example1.com/log/nginx.access.log;
 error_log   /var/www/example1.com/log/nginx_error.log debug;

 #set your default location
 location / {
  include proxy.conf;
  proxy_pass          http://backend;
 }
}
```

How it works...

In this configuration we set up an upstream, which is nothing but a set of servers with some proxy parameters. For the server `http://backend1.example1.com`, we have set a weight of five, which means that the majority of the requests will be directed to that server. This can be useful in cases where there are some powerful servers and some weaker ones. In the next server `http://backend2.example1.com`, we have set the parameters such that three failed requests over a time period of 30 seconds will result in the server being considered inoperative. The last one is a plain vanilla setup, where one error in a ten second window will make the server inoperative!

This displays the thought put in behind the design of Nginx. It seamlessly handles servers which are problematic and puts them in the set of inoperative servers. All requests to the server are sent in a round robin fashion. We will discuss modules in future recipes that ensure that the requests are sent using other queue mechanisms based on server load and other upstream server performance metrics.

Serving CGI files using thttpd and Nginx

At some point in time in Internet history, most applications were CGI based. Nginx does not serve CGI scripts, so the workaround is to use a really efficient and simple HTTP server called thttpd and to get Nginx to act as a proxy to it.

How to do it...

The best way to go about it is to set up thttpd from source code, apply the IP forwarding patch, and then to use the configuration below:

1. Download thttpd and apply the patch.

    ```
    wget http://www.acme.com/software/thttpd/thttpd-2.25b.tar.gz

    tar -xvzf  thttpd-2.25b.tar.gz
    ```

2. Save the code below in a file called `thttpd.patch`:

    ```
    --- thttpd-2.25b/libhttpd.c    2003-12-25 20:06:05.000000000 +0100
    +++ thttpd-2.25b-patched/libhttpd.c    2005-01-09
    00:26:04.867255248 +0100
    @@ -2207,6 +2207,12 @@
            if ( strcasecmp( cp, "keep-alive" ) == 0 )
                hc->keep_alive = 1;
            }
    +        else if ( strncasecmp( buf, "X-Forwarded-For:", 16 ) == 0
    )
    +        { // Use real IP if available
    +        cp = &buf[16];
    +        cp += strspn( cp, " \t" );
    +        inet_aton( cp, &(hc->client_addr.sa_in.sin_addr) );
    +                }
     #ifdef LOG_UNKNOWN_HEADERS
            else if ( strncasecmp( buf, "Accept-Charset:", 15 ) == 0
    ||
                strncasecmp( buf, "Accept-Language:", 16 ) == 0 ||
    ```

3. Apply the patch and install thttpd:

    ```
    patch -p 1 -i thttpd.patch

    cd thttpd-2.25b

    make

    sudo make install
    ```

4. Use the following configuration for `/etc/thttpd.conf`:

```
# BEWARE : No empty lines are allowed!
# This section overrides defaults
# This section _documents_ defaults in effect
# port=80
# nosymlink          # default = !chroot
# novhost
# nocgipat
# nothrottles
# host=0.0.0.0
# charset=iso-8859-1
host=127.0.0.1
port=8000
user=thttpd
logfile=/var/log/thttpd.log
pidfile=/var/run/thttpd.pid
dir=/var/www
cgipat=**.cgi|**.pl
```

5. Set up Nginx as a proxy for the port 8000.

```
server {
  listen    80;
  server_name  example1.com;
  access_log  /var/www/example1.com/log/nginx.access.log;
  error_log  /var/www/example1.com/log/nginx_error.log debug;

location /cgi-bin {
  include proxy.conf;
  proxy_pass        http://127.0.0.1:8000;
  }
}
```

How it works...

The setup above allows you to enjoy the best of CGI and Nginx. You initially set up thttpd, which will run on port 8000 of the server, which will effectively be the core CGI web server and you can run Nginx as the proxy for the user requests.

All you need to do is place the perl scripts in the `/var/www` directory and you will be running CGI using Nginx and thttpd.

You can also use the same technique as above to run CGI scripts using other CGI-capable servers like Apache and lightHTTPD as well. You will be required to change the operating ports of those servers to 8000 and the same configuration like above will work.

Setting up load balancing with reverse proxy

In most reverse proxy systems one wants to have some notion of load balancing in the system. In one of the preceding recipes, we have seen how to set up and run multiple upstream servers in a round robin mechanism of sending over the requests.

In this recipe, we will install a load balancing module which will allow us to set up a fair load balancing with the upstream servers.

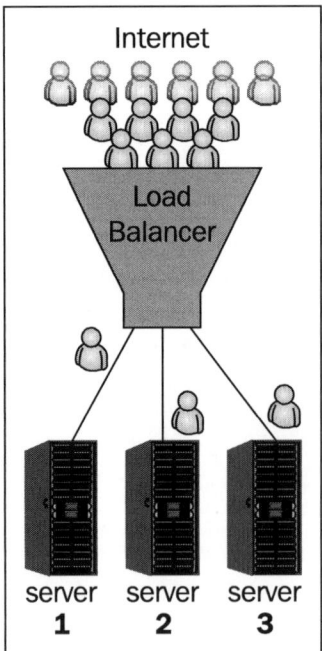

How to do it...

For this particular recipe we will install a third-party module called "upstream fair module".

1. You will need to go an download the module:

    ```
    wget https://github.com/gnosek/nginx-upstream-fair/tarball/master
    ```

2. Compile Nginx with the new module:

```
Tar -xvzf nginx-upstream-fair.tgz

Cd nginx

./configure --with-http_ssl_module --add-module=../nginx-upstream-fair/

Make && make install
```

3. You will need to add the following configuration to your `nginx.conf`:

```
upstream backend  {
  server backend1.example1.com;
  server backend2.example1.com;
  server backend3.example1.com;
  fair no_rr;
}

server {
 listen    80;
 server_name  example1.com;
 access_log  /var/www/example1.com/log/nginx.access.log;
 error_log  /var/www/example1.com/log/nginx_error.log debug;

 #set your default location
 location / {
  proxy_pass          http://backend;
 }
}
```

How it works...

This is a fairly straightforward setup once you understand the basics of setting up multiple upstream servers. In this particular "fair" mode, which is `no_rr`, the server will send the request to the first backend whenever it is idle. The goal of this module is to not send requests to already busy backends as it keeps information of how many requests a current backend is already processing. This is a much better model than the default round robin that is implemented in the default upstream directive.

There's more...

You can choose to run this load balancer module in a few other modes, as described below, based on your needs! This is a very simple way of ensuring that none of the backend experiences load unevenly as compared to the rest:

Mode	Meaning
default (that is fair;)	The default mode is a simple WLC-RR (weighted least-connection round-robin) algorithm with a caveat that the weighted part isn't actually too fair under low load.
no_rr	This means that whenever the first backend is idle, it's going to get the next request. If it's busy, the request will go to the second backend unless it's busy too, and so on.
weight_ mode=idle no_rr	This mode redefines the meaning of "idle". It now means "less than weight concurrent requests". So you can easily benchmark your backends and determine that **X** concurrent requests are the maximum for you.
weight_ mode=peak	This means that Nginx will never send more than weight requests to any single backend. If all backends are full, you will start receiving 502 errors.

Here is an example of a peak weight mode setup:

```
upstream backend  {
   server backend1.example1.com weight=4;
   server backend2.example1.com weight=3;
   server backend3.example1.com weight=4;
   fair weight_mode=idle no_rr;
}
```

Splitting requests based on various conditions using split-clients

This recipe will take a look at how we can potentially separate client requests based on various conditions that can arise.

We will also understand how we can potentially set up a simple page for A-B testing using this module.

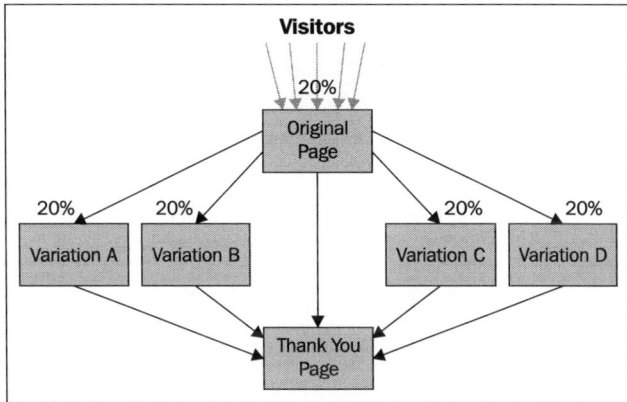

How to do it...

This module is fairly simple to use and comes inbuilt with Nginx. All you need to do is to insert the following configuration in your `nginx.conf`:

```
http {

    split-clients "${remote-addr}AAA" $variant {
        50.0% .one;
        50,0% .two;
        - "";
    }
...

server {
 listen    80;
 server_name   example1.com;
 access_log   /var/www/example1.com/log/nginx.access.log;
 error_log   /var/www/example1.com/log/nginx_error.log debug;

location / {
   root /var/www/example1.com;
   index index${variant}.html;
  }
 }
}
```

How it works...

This particular configuration sets up a system which is based upon the remote client address, assigns the values `.one`, `.two`, or "" to a variable `$variant`. Based upon the variable value, a different page is picked up from the file location.

The following table shows the various probabilities and actions from the above configuration:

Variable value	Probability	Page served
.one	50%	/var/www/example1.com/index.one.html
.two	50%	/var/www/example1.com/index.two.html
" "	0%	/var/www/example1.com/index.html

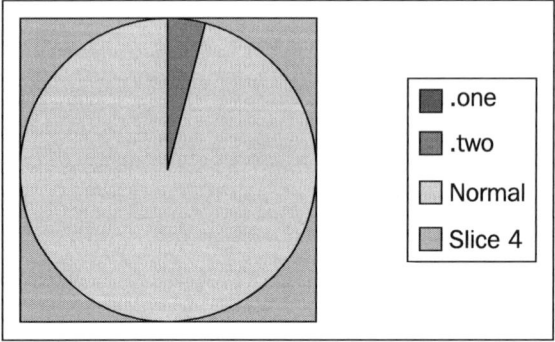

The preceding pie chart clearly displays the split across the two pages. Utilizing this approach, we are able to test out interactions with the page changes that you have made. This forms the basis of usability testing.

8
Improving Performance and SEO Using Nginx

In this chapter, we will cover:

- ► Setting up TCP options correctly for optimizing performance
- ► Reducing the keep-alives to free up Nginx workers
- ► Using Memcached as the cache backend
- ► Configuring the right event model and file limits
- ► Setting max-age expiry headers for client-side caching
- ► Blocking scrapers, bots, and spiders to save bandwidth
- ► Redirection of www to non-www domain for SEO
- ► Removing all white space from response
- ► Setting up server status for monitoring
- ► Setting up Munin for 24x7 Nginx monitoring
- ► Enabling GZIP pre-compression
- ► Preventing hotlinking using Nginx
- ► Using embedded Perl to minify JavaScript files
- ► Using embedded Perl to minify CSS files
- ► Using embedded Perl to serve sitemaps (SEO)
- ► Setting up Boost module on Drupal with Nginx

- ► Setting up streaming for Flash files
- ► Utilizing the 1x1 gif serving module to do offline processing

Introduction

This chapter is all about how you can make your site load faster and possibly get more traffic on your site. We will cover the basics of optimizing your Nginx setup and some SEO tricks. These techniques will not only be useful for your SEO, but also for the overall health of your site and applications.

Setting up TCP options correctly for optimizing performance

Nginx allows some easy ways to tweak TCP options which will be based upon your server operating system that will allow faster loading of your sites. We will have a look at the possible options and their impact.

How to do it...

The following configuration will optimize your setup for Linux:

```
user www-data;
worker_processes  1;

error_log  /var/log/nginx/error.log;
pid        /var/run/nginx.pid;

events {
    worker_connections  1024;
}

http {
    include        /etc/nginx/mime.types;
    default_type  application/octet-stream;

    access_log  /var/log/nginx/access.log;

    sendfile on;
    tcp_nodelay on;
    tcp_nopush off;
    ...
}
```

How it works...

We use the following directives, and in the following table we can see what they are actually utilized for:

Directive	Usage
`tcp_nodelay`	This directive allows or forbids the use of the socket option `TCP_NODELAY`. By definition, `TCP_NODELAY` is for a specific purpose; to disable the Nagle buffering algorithm. It should only be set for applications that send frequent small bursts of information without getting an immediate response; where timely delivery of data is required (the canonical example is mouse movements).
`tcp_nopush`	This directive permits or forbids the use of the socket options `TCP_NOPUSH` on FreeBSD or `TCP_CORK` on Linux. This option is only available when using sendfile. Setting this option causes Nginx to attempt to send it's HTTP response headers in one packet on Linux and FreeBSD 4.x On Linux, Nginx can use the `TCP_CORK` socket option. From the tcp(7) manual: `TCP_CORK` If set, don't send out partial frames. All queued partial frames are sent when the option is cleared again. This is useful for prepending headers before calling sendfile(2), or for throughput optimization. As currently implemented, there is a 200 millisecond ceiling on the time for which output is corked by `TCP_CORK`. If this ceiling is reached, then queued data is automatically transmitted. This option can be combined with `TCP_NODELAY` only since Linux 2.5.71. This option should not be used in code intended to be portable. On FreeBSD Nginx can use the `TCP_NOPUSH` socket option, which enables T/TCP transactions. This does much the same as the above, but is known to be slow and somewhat buggy on many versions of FreeBSD.

Reducing the keep-alives to free up Nginx workers

Are you starting to feel that a lot of your Nginx seems to be tied up without actually having a lot of traffic on you site? This simple tweak will let you efficiently utilize your Nginx setup when you feel that your users are spending a lot of time on a particular page before moving to the next page on your site.

How to do it...

This is, again, a fairly simple change in the configuration file as shown in the following code:

```
user www-data;
worker_processes  1;

error_log  /var/log/nginx/error.log;
pid        /var/run/nginx.pid;

events {
    worker_connections  1024;
}

http {
    include       /etc/nginx/mime.types;
    default_type  application/octet-stream;

    access_log  /var/log/nginx/access.log;

. . .
#keepalive_timeout  65;
keepalive_timeout  3;

. . .
}
```

How it works...

This simple directive actually sets the value of the time the connection with the client is kept alive after a request. For example, in the preceding setting the connection will wait for three seconds after serving a client request waiting for the next request from them (and in the process ignoring other clients).

The idea is finding the right amount of time after which if you close the connection, Nginx does not end up ignoring many requests unnecessarily. This will improve the efficiency of how connections are managed by Nginx.

Using Memcached as the cache backend

Over the last couple of years, Memcached has been one of the most utilized caching layers used by nearly every large portal. It is interesting to notice how every platform has evolved to support this as a default caching mechanism. Nginx is not far behind and can utilize all the power of Memcached as a caching backend.

How to do it...

The Memcached module is by default compiled into Nginx. In this we will assume that a local Memcached instance is running on the 11211 port. The following configuration will allow you to run a simple caching setup:

```
server {
  server_name www.example1.com;
  location / {
    set $memcached_key $uri;
    memcached_pass      127.0.0.1:11211;
    default_type        text/html;
    error_page          404 @fallback;
  }

  location @fallback {
    proxy_pass http://backend;
  }
}
```

How it works...

This is a fairly simple setup, where the complete site is cached in Memcached. The idea is that when Nginx is queried for a given URL, it is checked if Nginx has the corresponding page in memory or not. If it has, then it is served directly from there. Otherwise, we call the dynamic backend of the site.

The catch, however, is that you will need to save the outputs of the pages in memory for Nginx to be able to query it from Memcached. The following diagram is an example of how this works in practice with a framework such as Django (Python).

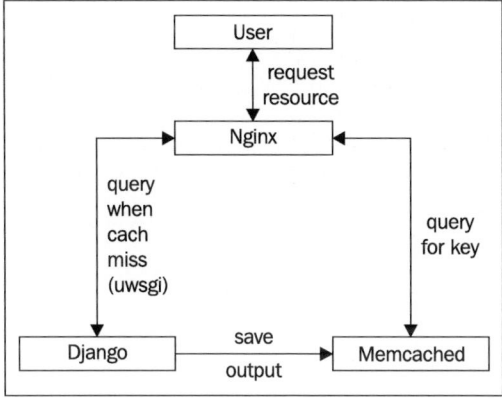

Configuring the right event model and file limits

Nginx is an event-driven web server and it always tries to use the underlying event model in the parent operating system to efficiently function. We will see the various choices on offer depending on the operating systems we operate in. In addition to that we will also have a look at how to modify the limits on file descriptor in the configuration.

How to do it...

This simple set of changes within the configuration is all that is needed to make changes in the event model and file limits. You will, however, need to also modify `sysctl.conf` on Linux and its equivalent on other operating systems to enhance the underlying file limits in place or the following setting will be ignored:

```
user www-data;
worker_processes   1;

worker_rlimit_nofile 206011;

error_log  /var/log/nginx/error.log;
pid        /var/run/nginx.pid;

events {
    event select;
worker_connections  1024;
}

http {

...

}
```

How it works...

In this current setup, we have set a fairly high limit on the number of open file descriptors that a worker process can have. We have also gone ahead and explicitly selected the select event model which comes built in by default in Nginx. You can also choose the poll event model or an alternative based upon the operating system you are on. The following table outlines the various options one has in selecting the event models.

Select method	Operating system	Notes
select	All	Standard method compiled in by default
poll	All	Standard method compiled in by default

Select method	Operating system	Notes
kqueue	FreeBSD 4.1+, OpenBSD 2.9+, NetBSD 2.0 and MacOS X	With dual-processor machines running MacOS X using kqueue can lead to kernel panic
epoll	Linux 2.6+	In some distributions, like SuSE 8.2, there are patches for supporting epoll by kernel version 2.4
rtsig	Linux 2.2.19+	By default no more than 1024 POSIX realtime (queued) signals can be outstanding in the entire system
/dev/poll	Solaris 7 11/99+, HP/UX 11.22+ (eventport), IRIX 6.5.15+ and Tru64 UNIX 5.1A+	
eventport	Solaris 10	To avoid kernel panic, it is necessary to install this security patch

Setting max-age expiry headers for client-side caching

In a reverse proxy setup, one of the most crucial tasks of a frontend web server like Nginx is to serve the static files. This is one of the most effective optimizations in the arsenal of a web administrator. In this, we set the client side cache expiry on static files to a significantly high value far in the future. This ensures that if the site is frequently used by the user, the static files like the images, CSS, and JavaScript files are not downloaded once again. This leads to a significantly better interaction with the site.

If you tend to use development plugins such as Firebug (which you can check out at `http://getfirebug.com`), they show you the headers of the files downloaded when you load a page, as shown in the following screenshot. This shows an example of the CSS files downloaded on the Yahoo! site:

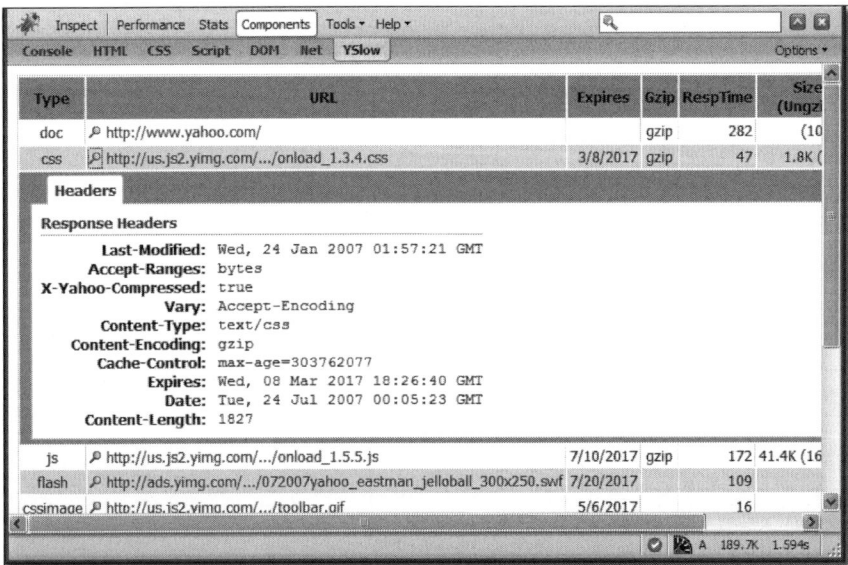

How to do it...

This is a simple configuration change that needs to be made to the location directive that serves the static files:

```
location ~* \.(jpg|jpeg|gif|css|png|js|ico|html)$ {
        expires max;
}
location / {
  ...
  proxy_pass http://backend;
}
```

How it works...

This is a fairly simple directive where if the file is a static file like a CSS, JS, or any image file, we simply send the file back with the `Expires` header set far in the future. This will ensure that the file stays in the cache of the client browser and is not reloaded unnecessarily when the user comes back to the same page in the future.

Static files like these do not change on most sites, while the HTML which defines the structure of the content may be very much dynamic. This also prevents significant unnecessary bandwidth usage for the site owners.

 You must keep in mind that a lot of time you will need to modify static files, so in those cases you will need to append a random/different query string variable to force the client to download the fresh version of the static file.

Blocking scrapers, bots, and spiders to save bandwidth

If you have ever gone through your access log you will see a whole load of rather weird looking User-Agents visiting your site. Except for the larger search engines such as Google, Microsoft Bing, and Yahoo! every other bot is pretty much unnecessary in the larger scheme of the global SEO scenario today. In this recipe we will end up blocking out a whole lot of other content leechers and in the process save you valuable bandwidth.

This will also block a whole load of commenting bots that end up pushing ugly and unnecessary comments to screw up your site.

How to do it...

You will need to add the following in the location directive to keep away a fairly large list of scrapers, bots, and spiders. We will start with a smaller set of user agents to block, and can add others once we are sure of how it works.

```
location / {
    ...

if ($http_user_agent ~* aesop_com_spiderman|alexibot|backweb|bandit|ba
tchftp|bigfoot|black.?hole|blackwidow|blowfish|botalot|buddy|builtbott
ough|bullseye|cheesebot|cherrypicker|chinaclaw|collector|copier|copyri
ghtcheck|cosmos|crescent|curl|custo|da|diibot|disco|dittospyder|dragon
fly|drip|easydl|ebingbong|ecatch|eirgrabber) {

    rewrite ^/ http://www.example1.com/robots.txt;
}
proxy_pass http://backend;
}
```

How it works...

This set of rules effectively look at the HTTP user agent and compare it to a list "of know rouge" user agent list and reject the request by redirecting them to the `robots.txt` file. This also ensures that you are never wasting computation time and bandwidth on bots which can be utilized in providing a better quality of service for your users.

By stopping spam comments on your site, you are also effectively ensuring that your SEO does not get affected by pornographic or explicit content injected by them.

Redirection of www to non-www domain for SEO

Most people do not realize that `www.example1.com` is not the same as `example1.com` for the search engines. Technically, they are completely separate entities. All search engines have algorithms to detect copied content to rank out the people who plagiarize content. In such a situation it is imperative that people actually use either `www.example1.com` or `example1.com` as the operative domain name for their site.

The verdict on what is better depends on the use case; the puritans argue that www version represents the correct sub-domain for all the Internet users. It can be argued that in an age where we use acronyms for nearly every word, the extra characters are unnecessary and may even affect your site's popularity. In this recipe, we will stick with non-www as the primary domain and force all www pages to redirect to the non-www pages.

How to do it...

We will insert the following configuration in the http directive to redirect all `http://example1.com` requests to `http://www.example1.com`:

```
server {
    listen 80;
    server_name example1.com;
    location / {
        ...
    }
}
server {
    listen 80;
    server_name www.example1.com;
    rewrite ^ http://example1.com$uri permanent;
}
```

How it works...

This is a simple rewrite rule for all www based requests, where they are redirected to the non-www URL. This makes sure that there is only one version of a page visible on the Internet for the search engines to crawl.

Removing all white space from response

This may sound a bit absurd, but white spaces form a major chunk of the files being transferred on a site. It can be said that if you are using GZIP compression then it is not an issue, but if you are looking at getting the most out of your setup then every little thing matters. This recipe will help you strip out all the unnecessary white space without wasting precious development time doing the same.

How to do it...

This simple directive will allow you to strip the HTML served of white spaces. You will first need to install the `mod_strip` module.

1. You will first need to download the module and untar it:

   wget http://wiki.nginx.org/File:Mod_strip-0.1.tar.gz

   tar -xvzf Mod_strip-0.1.tar.gz

2. We then compile into Nginx the module, using the following configure statement:

   ./configure -add-module=../Mod_strip-0.1

   make && make install

3. We then put the following directive in the location part of the site that we want to strip spaces for:

   ```
   location / {
       strip on;
       . . .
       proxy_pass http://backend;
   }
   ```

How it works...

This is an extremely fast module and it efficiently removes all whitespaces (spaces, tabs, and newlines) from the HTML served by Nginx. This in combination with the GZIP compression provides quite a drastic improvement in page loading times.

Setting up server status for monitoring

Sometimes in an active production environment, it is not possible to process logs to see web server statistics on the fly. In such situations, Nginx provides you with a simple server status page. This page will give you enough information to understand the current load on the server.

How to do it...

This module does not come compiled in by default, so we will initially compile in the module and then configure the server status stub.

1. You will need to recompile Nginx and add the following flag to the configure option:

   ```
   ./configure --with-http_stub_status_module
   make && make install
   ```

2. Then we will go ahead and use the configuration to add a new status end-point:

   ```
   location /nginx_status {
     stub_status on;
     access_log    off;
   }
   ```

How it works...

This simple configuration will create a page `http://www.example1.com/nginx_status`, which will give you statistics on how much load is there on your web server. The following is an example of what you may get to see on the page.

We can also set up access control for this page by looking at the *Setting up HTTP auth for access control* recipe in *Chapter 5, Let's Be Secure: Security Modules* which will let you set up HTTP authentication.

```
Active connections: 291
server accepts handled requests
  16630948 16630948 31070465
Reading: 6 Writing: 179 Waiting: 106
```

The following table explains the meaning of the server status output.

Statistic	Meaning
Active connections	Number of open connections to the backend
Server accepts handled requests	Nginx accepted 16630948 connections, went ahead and handled 16630948 connections and served 31070465 requests
Reading	The number of requests Nginx is reading

Statistic	Meaning
Writing	The requests that are being processed or being written back to the clients
Waiting	Connections that are kept alive with the clients (KeepAlives)

Setting up Munin for 24x7 Nginx monitoring

In a production level environment where you may have multiple servers running, it becomes necessary to have top level monitoring tools such as Munin. The tools let you collate information and figure out load levels on the fly thus keeping you in the loop 24 hours, seven days a week. This recipe aims at being useful for the new Nginx user as well as highly experienced system administrators. The following screenshot is a sample of the kind of visualizations Munin generates:

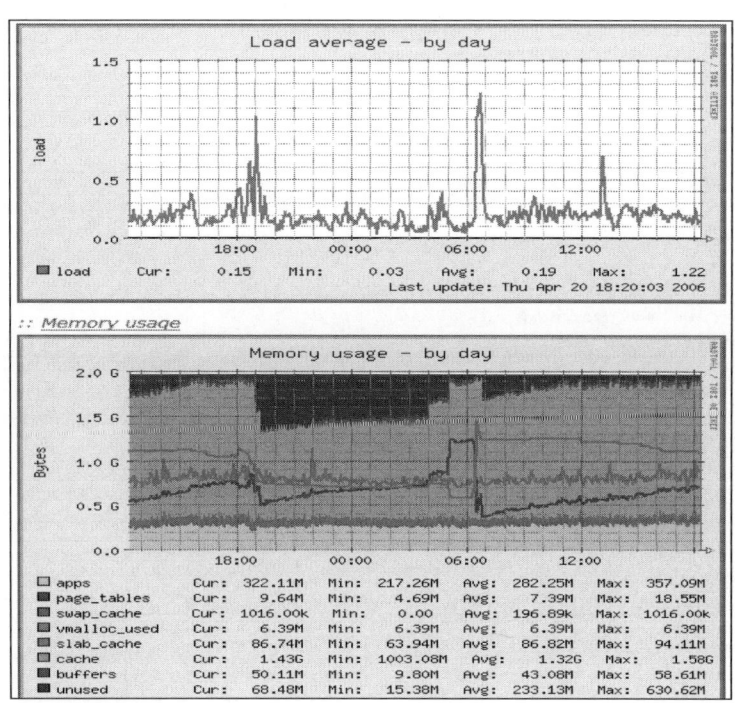

How to do it...

There are two parts to this recipe; the first is in setting up Nginx with the server stub module.

1. You will need to recompile Nginx and add the following flag to the configure option:

   ```
   ./configure --with-http_stub_status_module
   Make && make install
   ```

2. Then we will go ahead and use the configuration to add a new status end-point:

```
location /nginx_status {
  stub_status on;
  access_log   off;
}
```

Now we will go ahead and install the Munin plugins. Do note that we are assuming that you have already set up Munin on your system.

1. You will first download the plugins:

```
cd /usr/share/munin/plugins
```

```
sudo wget -O nginx_request http://exchange.munin-monitoring.org/
plugins/nginx_request/version/2/download
```

```
sudo wget -O nginx_status http://exchange.munin-monitoring.org/
plugins/nginx_status/version/3/download
```

```
sudo wget -O nginx_memory http://exchange.munin-monitoring.org/
plugins/nginx_memory/version/1/download
```

```
sudo chmod +x nginx_request
```

```
sudo chmod +x nginx_status
```

```
sudo chmod +x nginx_memory
```

2. Now we will link the plugins to the correct directories:

```
sudo ln -s /usr/share/munin/plugins/nginx_request /etc/munin/
plugins/nginx_request
```

```
sudo ln -s /usr/share/munin/plugins/nginx_status /etc/munin/
plugins/nginx_status
```

```
sudo ln -s /usr/share/munin/plugins/nginx_memory /etc/munin/
plugins/nginx_memory
```

3. Add the Nginx server stub URL to the Munin configuration (/etc/munin/plugin-conf.d/munin-node).

```
[nginx*]
env.url http://localhost/nginx_status
```

4. Restart the munin-node:

```
sudo /etc/init.d/munin-node restart
```

Now you should be able to view something like the following screenshot on your Munin installation:

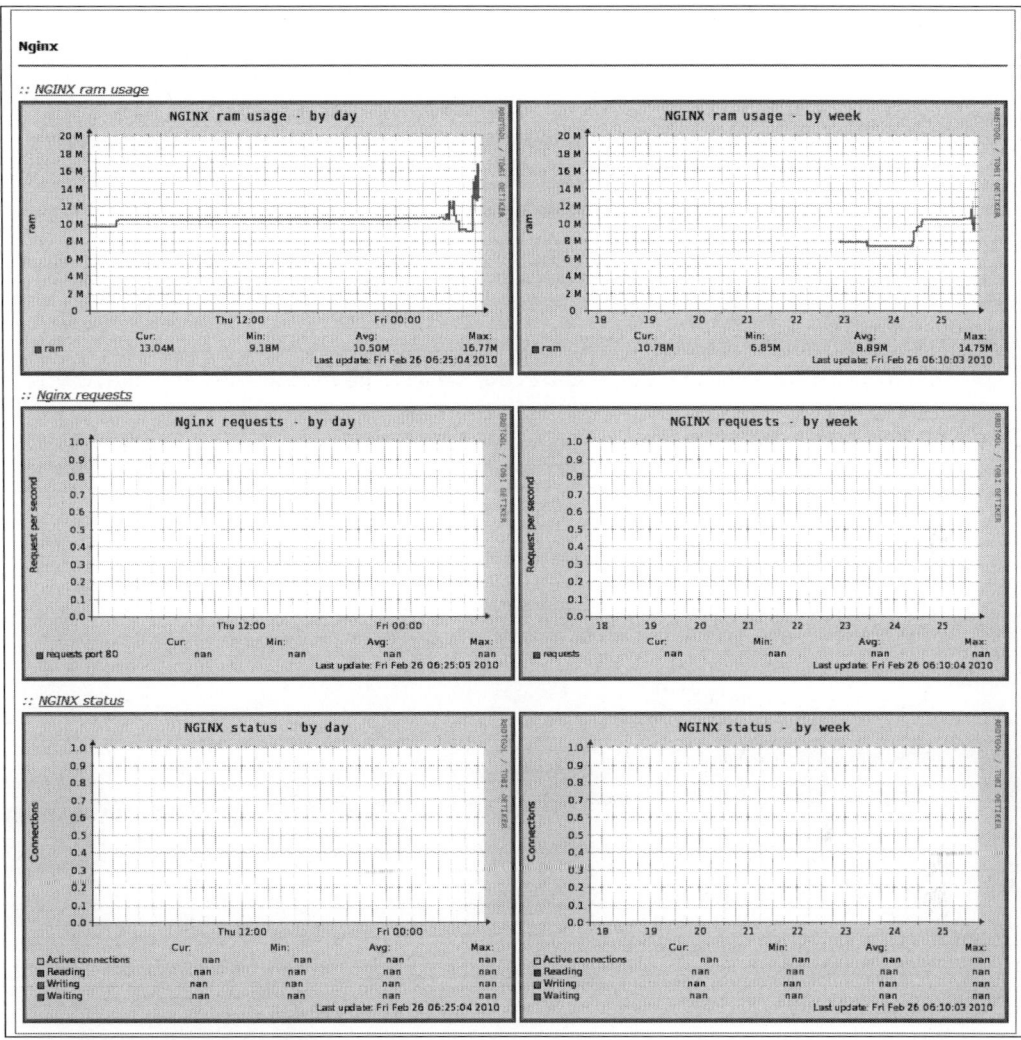

How it works...

This two part setup first installs the server status stub module for Nginx which is used by Munin to keep track of the server loads. In the second part, we install the various Munin plugins that are needed to effectively monitor Nginx. Munin will keep polling the server status and parse it to gather the relevant information to generate the graphs. These simple visualizations can help the system administrator optimize the system further and potentially plan future hardware needs based on projections.

Enabling GZIP pre-compression

We have had a look at how GZIP compression can lower the site's loading time drastically. We can further extend that thinking by pre-compressing the static sites that we want to serve and effectively reduce the computation power we waste to compress the file each and every time. This recipe will automagically help you serve a pre-compressed gzipped version of your static file.

How to do it...

You will need to carry out the following steps to enable gzip pre-compression module and use it effectively.

1. You will need to recompile Nginx and add the following flag to the configure option:

   ```
   ./configure --with-http_gzip_static_module
   Make && make install
   ```

2. Now, you will need to compress the various static files (using the gzip command line utility, if on UNIX) that you have so that Nginx can serve those pre-compressed ones whenever possible. Make sure that the compressed files are placed in the same directory as the original files.

3. Make the following changes to the Nginx configuration file:

   ```
   http {
   . . .

   gzip_static on;

   gzip_http_version    1.1;
   gzip_proxied         expired no-cache no-store private auth;
   gzip_disable         "MSIE [1-6]\.";
   gzip_vary            on;
   ```

How it works...

When this module is turned on, Nginx will always look for a pre-compressed file whenever a file is being served from the disk. The idea is to simply avoid spending more CPU time compressing the content every time.

Preventing hotlinking using Nginx

A lot of multimedia driven sites have the problem of people linking and embedding their content without their explicit permission. This not only leads to copyright issues at times, but also ends up in lost bandwidth for the site minus the traffic. This is clearly not a good scenario for any site. This recipe helps you prevent this situation on your site.

How to do it...

This simple rule will stop other sites from linking to your content:

```
server {

server_name www.example1.com;

location ~* ^.+\.(jpg|jpeg|gif)$ {
    valid_referers none blocked example1.com www.example1.com;
    if ($invalid_referer) {
        return 444;
    }
}
}

...

}
```

How it works...

The idea behind this is to set a list of correct referrer values which are permissible. The rest are rejected. In case there is no match with this list the variable, `$invalid_referer` is set to 1. The lists of parameters in the `valid_referers` mean the following:

parameter	Meaning
None	This value implies that it is a match when the "refers" line is not a part of the request header.
blocked	This means masked refer headers by firewall. For example "Referer : XXXXXX".

Do note that this method is not an absolute fix for hot-linking as it is fairly easy to spoof the header.

Using embedded Perl to minify JavaScript files

This recipe will have a look at how to get embedded Perl working in Nginx and use it to minify JavaScript files. The basic concept of minifying JavaScript files is to reduce the size of the file by removing unnecessary whitespaces and shortening variable names. Of course, any compression of the JavaScript file should not be affecting the actual functionality of the site.

How to do it...

We will start by installing the embedded Perl module and then go ahead and configure the setup to minify the JavaScript files.

1. You will need to recompile Nginx and add the following flag to the configure option:

    ```
    ./configure -with-http_perl_module
    Make && make install
    ```

2. You will need to add the following into your Nginx configuration to get started with using embedded Perl. This assumes that you have installed the JavaScript minifier library from CPAN:

    ```
    http {
      perl_modules perl;
      perl_require Javascript/Minifier.pm;
      perl_require Minify.pm;
      root /var/www;
      server {
        server_name www.example1.com;
        location / {
          index   index.html index.htm;
        }
        location ~ \.js$ {
          perl Minify::handler;
        }
      }
    }
    ```

3. You will then need to create the Minify handler which will reside in the `Minify.pm` file. This is the actual function that will minify the JavaScript code and cache, and serve the generated file.

    ```
    package Minify;
    use nginx;
    use JavaScript::Minifier qw(minify);
    ```

```perl
sub handler {
  my $r=shift;
  my $cache_dir="/tmp";  # Cache directory where minified files
will be kept
  my $cache_file=$r->uri;
  $cache_file=~s!/!_!g;
  $cache_file=join("/", $cache_dir, $cache_file);
  my $uri=$r->uri;
  my $filename=$r->filename;

  return DECLINED unless -f $filename;

  if (! -f $cache_file) {
    open(INFILE, $filename) or die "Error reading file: $!";
    open(OUTFILE, '>' . $cache_file ) or die "Error writting file:
$!";
    minify(input => *INFILE, outfile => *OUTFILE);
    close(INFILE);
    close(OUTFILE);
  }
  $r->sendfile($cache_file);
  return OK;
}
1;

__END__
```

4. Now you can simply go ahead and restart Nginx. You will begin to notice minified JavaScript files appearing in your /tmp directory.

How it works...

This is a fairly interesting and simple setup, where we basically use embedded Perl as a way of minifying the JavaScript files and caching them. The Perl script is intelligent in the way that it ensures that the minifying happens only once initially, and then after every request the file is served from the hard drive.

A comparison of the various Yahoo UI JavaScript files when minified can be seen in the following screenshot:

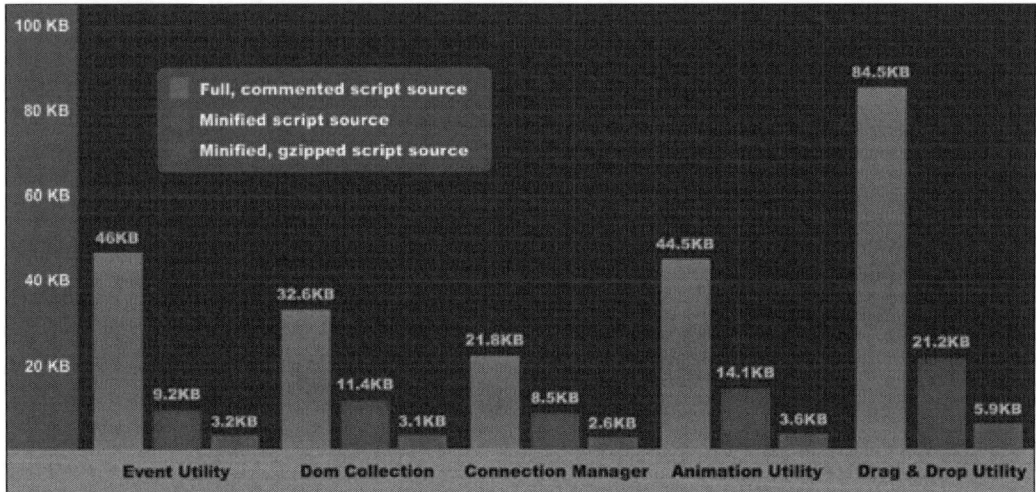

There's more...

This same approach can be used to do a whole lot of other utility activities inside the web server. We will have a look at how to minify CSS in the next recipe using a very similar approach.

Using embedded Perl to minify CSS files

We will have a look at how we can minify CSS files using embedded Perl within Nginx. This simple recipe will ensure that you do not waste time thinking about such optimizations when deploying a production site. Minifying CSS can result in significantly smaller asset files which need to be downloaded by the end user.

How to do it...

We will start by installing the embedded Perl module and then going ahead to configure the setup to minify the JavaScript files.

1. You will need to recompile Nginx and add the following flag to the configure option:

   ```
   ./configure --with-http_perl_module
   Make && make install
   ```

2. You will need to add the following into your Nginx configuration to get started with using embedded Perl. This assumes that you have installed the CSS minifier library from CPAN:

```
http {
  perl_modules perl;
  perl_require CSS/Minifier.pm;
  perl_require Minify.pm;
  root /var/www;
  server {
    location / {
      index  index.html index.htm;
    }
    location ~ \.css$  {
      perl Minify::handler;
    }
  }
}
```

3. You will then need to create the Minify handler, which will reside in the `Minify.pm` file. This is the actual function that will minify the code and cache, and serve the generated CSS file:

```perl
package Minify;
use nginx;
use CSS::Minifier qw(minify);
sub handler {
  my $r=shift;
  my $cache_dir="/tmp";  # Cache directory where minified files
will be kept
  my $cache_file=$r->uri;
  $cache_file=~s!/!_!g;
  $cache_file=join("/", $cache_dir, $cache_file);
  my $uri=$r->uri;
  my $filename=$r->filename;

  return DECLINED unless -f $filename;

  if (! -f $cache_file) {
    open(INFILE, $filename) or die "Error reading file: $!";
    open(OUTFILE, '>' . $cache_file ) or die "Error writting file:
$!";
    minify(input => *INFILE, outfile => *OUTFILE);
    close(INFILE);
    close(OUTFILE);
  }
  $r->sendfile($cache_file);
  return OK;
}
1;
__END__
```

4. Now you can simply go ahead and restart Nginx. You will start to notice minified CSS files appearing in your /tmp directory.

How it works...

In this recipe, we first ensure that you install the embedded Perl module. Then we configure Nginx to run a piece of Perl code when a CSS file is queried for. The Perl script effectively minifies the CSS file on the first call made, and it serves the minified file from the caching location for subsequent calls.

Using embedded Perl to serve sitemaps (SEO)

Since the advent of search engines, SEO has played a crucial role in the Internet economy. Businesses want to attract more visitors to their sites, thus creating more awareness and opportunities to sell their products/services. One of the most basic concepts that have served as standard for search engines when they index a site for information is the sitemap. A sitemap is nothing but a directory of all the potential links on the site. It also assigns weights to how often a particular page changes, ensuring that a search engine can come back and look at the page at regular intervals.

We will look at how to take your sitemaps and serve them correctly using Nginx. You can then use these sitemaps on the various webmaster tools provided by Google, Bing, and other search engines.

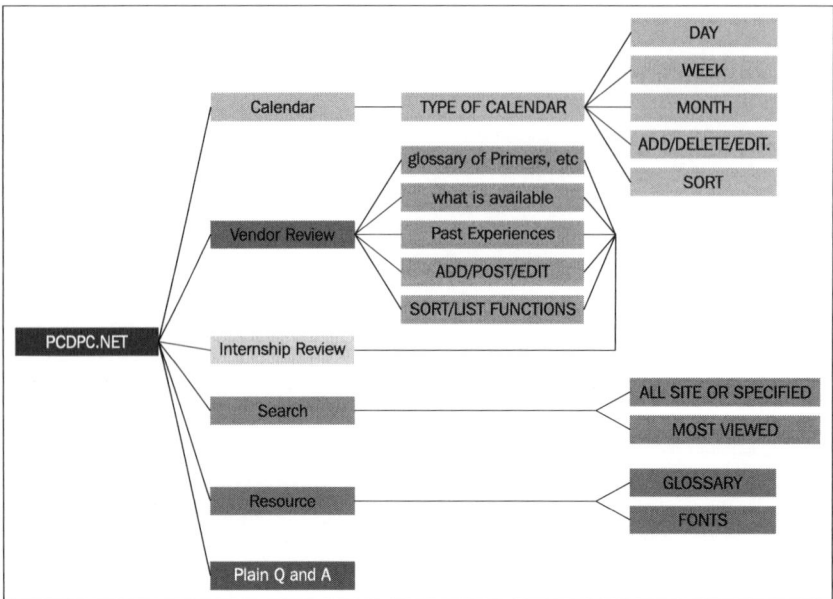

How to do it...

In this recipe we will first set up a sitemap generator and then integrate it with our Nginx setup to generate and serve sitemaps correctly.

1. In this we will assume that you are able to set up the python sitemap generator: (`http://sitemap-generators.googlecode.com/svn/trunk/docs/en/ sitemap-generator.html`).

2. You can now go ahead and put the following configuration into your Nginx setup to enable the sitemap generation:

```
http {
    include        mime.types;
    default_type   application/octet-stream;

    perl_modules perl;
    perl_require Sitemap.pm;

    keepalive_timeout   65;

    server {
        listen         80;
        server_name    www.example1.com;

        location / {
            root    html;
            index   index.html index.htm;
        }
        location /sitemap.xml {
            perl Sitemap::handler;
        }
    }
}
```

3. Now we need to place the Perl handler, which will allow you to serve the generated sitemaps:

```
package Sitemap;
use nginx;
use LWP::Simple;

our $basedir="/var/www/www.example1.com";

sub handler {
    my $r=shift;
    my $cache_dir="/tmp";   # Cache directory where minified files
will be kept
    my $cache_file=$r->uri;
    $cache_file=~s!/!_!g;
    $cache_file=join("/", $cache_dir, $cache_file);
```

```
my $uri=$r->uri;
my $filename=$r->filename;

return DECLINED unless -f $filename;

if (! -f $cache_file) {
   `python sitemap_gen.py` # Assumes that google sitemap
generator is in the same directory
   }
   $r->sendfile($cache_file);
   return OK;

}

1;

__END__
```

4. Now all you need is to restart Nginx and visit `http://www.example1.com/sitemap.xml`.

How it works...

This is a fairly interesting setup that basically sets up the Google sitemap generator and then utilizes it when the sitemap is queried for by the search engines. The Perl code is fairly simple as it is only called when the sitemap is not found. It basically makes a call to the python code, which will generate the sitemap and go ahead and serve the files.

Setting up Boost module on Drupal with Nginx

Drupal is one of the leading open source CMS applications out there. It has proved to be extremely capable in handling a variation of content driven portals out on the Internet today and will continue to be a dominant player in this market. As with any high performance platform, a particular module called Boost has emerged as a strong tool in the hands of system administrators who want to scale up and optimize their Drupal setup. In this recipe, we will look at how we can take a Drupal setup which has Boost, and use Nginx's strength of serving static files for a fairly significant optimization.

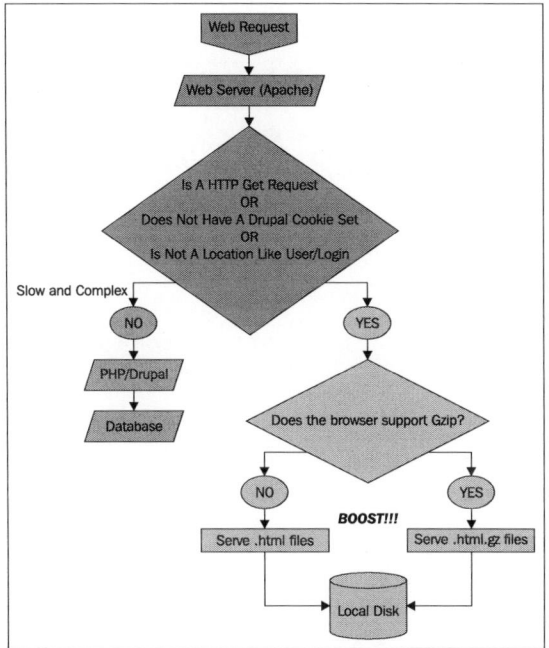

How to do it...

It is assumed that you have already installed and configured Boost for Drupal. It is a fairly simple and well-documented setup which can be found online (`http://drupal.org/project/boost`).

1. Now that you have already installed Boost and Nginx is running as your frontend web server and using PHP-FCGI, you will need to place the following configuration in your Nginx sites-enabled directory:

```
server {
    listen  80;
    server_name  example1.com;
    access_log /var/log/nginx/example1.com.access.log;
    error_log /var/log/nginx/example1.com.error.log;
    root /var/www/example1.com;
    index index.php;

    location / {
        rewrite ^/(.*)/$ /$1 permanent; # remove trailing slashes
        try_files $uri @cache;
    }
    location @cache {
        if ( $request_method !~ GET ) {
```

```
            return 405;
        }
        if ($http_cookie ~ "DRUPAL_UID") {
            return 405;
        }
        error_page 405 = @drupal;

        expires epoch;
        add_header Cache-Control "must-revalidate, post-check=0,
pre-check=0";
        charset utf-8;

        try_files /cache/$host${uri}_$args.html @drupal;
    }
    location @drupal {
        rewrite ^/(.*)$ /index.php?q=$1 last;
    }
    location ~* (/\..*|settings\.php$|\.(htaccess|engine|inc|info|
install|module|profile|pl|po|sh|.*sql|theme|tpl(\.php)?|xtmpl)$|^(
Entries.*|Repository|Root|Tag|Template))$ {
        deny all;
    }
    location ~ \.php$ {
        try_files $uri @drupal;
        fastcgi_pass 127.0.0.1:9000;
        fastcgi_index index.php;
        fastcgi_param SCRIPT_FILENAME $document_root$fastcgi_
script_name;
        include /etc/nginx/fastcgi_params;
    }
    location ~ \.css$ {
        if ( $request_method !~ GET ) {
            return 405;
        }
        if ($http_cookie ~ "DRUPAL_UID") {
            return 405;
        }
        error_page 405 = @uncached;

        access_log  off;
        expires  max; #if using aggregator

        try_files /cache/$host${uri}_.css $uri =404;
    }
    location ~ \.js$ {
        if ( $request_method !~ GET ) {
```

```
                return 405;
        }
        if ($http_cookie ~ "DRUPAL_UID") {
                return 405;
        }
        error_page 405 = @uncached;

        access_log  off;
        expires  max; # if using aggregator

        try_files /cache/$host${uri}_.js $uri =404;
    }

    location @uncached {
        access_log  off;
        expires  max;
    }

    location ~* ^.+\.(jpg|jpeg|gif|png|ico)$ {
        if ($http_referer !~ ^(http://example1.com) ) { # prevent
image hijacking
            return 444;
        }

        access_log        off;
        expires           45d;

        try_files $uri =404;
    }
}
```

2. All you need to do now is restart Nginx.

How it works...

This particular configuration can be looked at in the following steps. First, when the request comes in, the Boost physical cache it is checked. If it is found in the cache, it is served back to the client. If not, it basically rewrites the clean URL into the Drupal `index.php` argument form and makes the PHP call.

This is a highly optimized setup, as it ensures that you serve the static files using Nginx whenever possible. As generating similar pages consistently is clearly a waste of precious server resources, this will let you focus on optimizing more frontend aspects of your web application.

Setting up streaming for Flash files

Video has become quite the dominant format on the net. It is also fair to say that Flash has been the driving force behind this over the last couple of years. YouTube (http://youtube. com) is a good example of FLV streaming video sites. In this recipe, we will look at how simple it is to set up Flash video streaming.

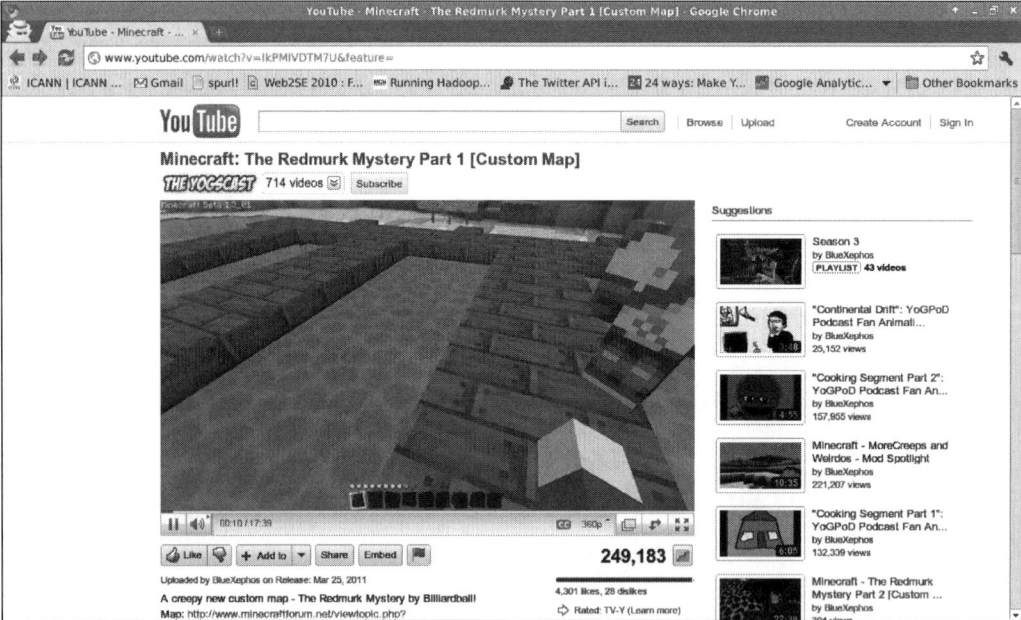

How to do it...

In this simple recipe, you will initially need to re-compile Nginx with the FLV module and then configure the directories that will serve the FLV files.

1. You will need to recompile Nginx and add the following flag to the configure option:

    ```
    ./configure --with-http_flv_module

    Make && make install
    ```

2. You will then need to add the following configuration to the directory location where you are streaming it from:

    ```
    location ~ \.flv$ {
      flv;
    }
    ```

3. You will then need to restart Nginx.

How it works...

This is a fairly simple setup where you will not need to do a lot to get FLV streaming working in no time. This module allows you to seek within FLV files using time-based offsets. This means that the user is able to start the video from somewhere in the middle and perform other similar video timeline operations.

Utilizing the 1x1 GIF serving module to do offline processing

Sometimes we encounter situations where the backend processing takes a bit more time than necessary and the client has to unnecessarily wait for a response. This recipe looks into a way of making a non-block call to a URL, potentially allowing you to send a response back to the user's browser that much faster, and yet ensuring that the background processing occurs.

It is also used for delivering an empty GIF which can be used for spacing in table-based HTML design.

How to do it...

All you need to implement a simple example is to use the following configuration:

```
upstream backend {
. . .
}
server {
server_name www.example1.com;
. . .
location / {
    empty_gif;
    post_action /post;
}
location = /post {
    internal;
    proxy_pass http://backend;
}
}
```

How it works...

This is a simple example where a 1x1 GIF is returned immediately when someone visits the site `http://www.example1.com`. That, in turn, actually fires up a POST call on `http://www.example1.com/post`, which is an internal only call. This web server call will perform whatever background activity is required, while the client would have already received his 200OK response.

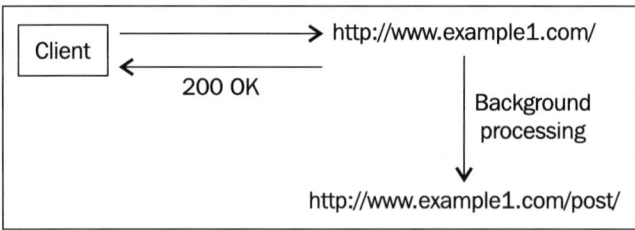

9
Using Other Third-party Modules

In this chapter, we will cover:

- ▶ Setting up an IMAP/POP3 proxy server
- ▶ Setting up authentication for mail services
- ▶ Setting up SSL for mail authentication
- ▶ Using Nginx as a WEBDAV reverse proxy
- ▶ Dynamic image resizing using Nginx
- ▶ Replacing and searching text in Nginx response
- ▶ Assembling ZIP files on the fly
- ▶ Using Nginx as a HTTP publish-subscribe server
- ▶ Transforming XML responses using XSLT templates
- ▶ Setting up Etags for static content
- ▶ Easy logging of page load times
- ▶ Streaming of MP4/H.264 files
- ▶ Setting up SCGI sites
- ▶ Setting up expiring links

Introduction

This chapter will have a look at some inbuilt, third-party modules which allow us to extend and use Nginx with other protocols, such as IMAP, POP3, WebDAV, and much more. Due to the flexible and well-defined module API, many module developers have used Nginx for interesting web-based tasks, such as XSLT transformations, image resizing, and HTTP publish-subscribe server.

Setting up an IMAP/POP3 proxy server

One of the most understated uses of Nginx is that of acting as a mail proxy server. It understands the IMAP, SMTP, and the POP3 protocols. In this recipe we will set up Nginx as a proxy for your test IMAP/POP3 server. However, you will need to have an authentication script that will basically return a response redirecting the incoming client to its correct IMAP or POP3 server.

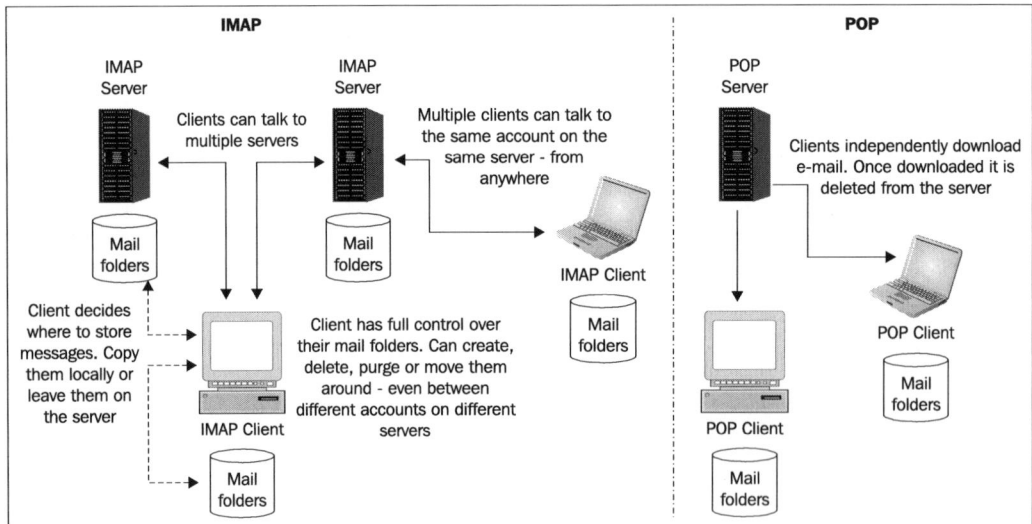

How to do it...

You need to put the following configuration in your setup:

```
mail {
  auth_http   localhost:9000/cgi-bin/auth;

  proxy   on;

  imap_capabilities   "IMAP4rev1"   "UIDPLUS";
  server {
    listen      143;
    protocol    imap;
```

```
    server_name imap.example1.com;
}

pop3_capabilities   "TOP"   "USER";
server {
    listen      110;
    protocol    pop3;
    server_name pop3.example1.com;
}
}
```

How it works...

This setup takes any incoming request and sends back a response outlining the POP3 or IMAP server it must connect with. We can see the necessary capabilities that the connecting client must have in order to work with the POP3 or IMAP server.

The auth endpoint will return something as follows:

```
HTTP/1.0 200 OK
Auth-Status: OK
Auth-Server: 192.168.1.10
Auth-Port: 110
Auth-User: newname
```

This basically tells the client that they need to connect with 192.168.1.10 on port 110 to continue further interaction with the backend POP3 server.

Setting up authentication for mail services

Mail being a personal form of communication inevitably requires authentication of some form or another. We will use embedded Perl to do the authentication in this example. This is driven in the backend with a table that contains the user and corresponding mail server list.

How to do it...

All you need to enable IMAP and POP3 support is to paste the following configuration in your Nginx setup:

```
user   nobody;
worker_processes   1;
error_log   logs/error.log   info;
pid         logs/nginx.pid;

events {
    worker_connections   1024;
```

```
      multi_accept on;
    }
  http {
    perl_modules  perl/lib;
    perl_require  mailauth.pm;

    server {
      location /auth {
        perl  mailauth::handler;
      }
    }
  }
  mail {
    auth_http  127.0.0.1:80/auth;

    pop3_capabilities  "TOP"  "USER";
    imap_capabilities  "IMAP4rev1"  "UIDPLUS";

    server {
      listen      110;
      protocol    pop3;
      proxy       on;
    }

    server {
      listen      143;
      protocol    imap;
      proxy       on;
    }
```

Now you will also need to create a file called `mailauth.pm` in the configuration directory and paste the following code:

```
package mailauth;
use nginx;
use DBI;
my $dsn="DBI:mysql:database=DBNAME;host=HOSTNAME";
our $dbh=DBI->connect_cached($dsn, 'dbusername', 'dbpass', {AutoCommit
=> 1});
our $sth=$dbh->prepare("select password,mail_server from mailaccounts
where username=? limit 1");

our $auth_ok;
our $mail_server_ip={};
our $protocol_ports={};
$mail_server_ip->{'mailhost01'}="192.168.1.22";
$mail_server_ip->{'mailhost02'}="192.168.1.33";
$protocol_ports->{'pop3'}=110;
```

```perl
$protocol_ports->{'imap'}=143;
sub handler {
  my $r = shift;
  $auth_ok=0;

  $sth->execute($r->header_in("Auth-User"));
  my $hash=$sth->fetchrow_hashref();
  # assuming that the query results password and mail_server
  # assuming that the password is in crypt format

  if (crypt($r->header_in("Auth-Pass"), $hash->{'password'}) eq
$r->header_in("Auth-Pass")){
    $auth_ok=1;
  }
  if ($auth_ok==1){
    $r->header_out("Auth-Status", "OK") ;
    $r->header_out("Auth-Server", $mail_server_ip->{$hash->{'mail_
server'}});
    $r->header_out("Auth-Port", $protocol_ports->{$r->header_in("Auth-
Protocol")});
  } else {
    $r->header_out("Auth-Status", "Invalid login or password") ;
  }

  $r->send_http_header("text/html");

  return OK;
}
1;

__END__
```

How it works...

The preceding configuration basically works in the following way; the authorization information is passed in the header to the proxy.

```
GET /auth HTTP/1.0
Host: auth.server.hostname
Auth-Method: plain
Auth-User: user
Auth-Pass: password
Auth-Protocol: imap
Auth-Login-Attempt: 1
Client-IP: 192.168.1.1
```

Then the Perl code will actually verify the information in the header, and based on the protocol it will choose the mail server it needs to redirect to. The end-point then sends back the following on the success of the request; this will be the backend that the service will connect to.

```
HTTP/1.0 200 OK
Auth-Status: OK
Auth-Server: 192.168.1.22
Auth-Port: 110
Auth-User: newname
```

Setting up SSL for mail authentication

This recipe will look at how one can set up SSL for the mail proxy you have working with Nginx. This will add a significant layer of security to the initial authentication exchange, which would happen in plain text and would be exposed to the man in the middle and replay attacks easily.

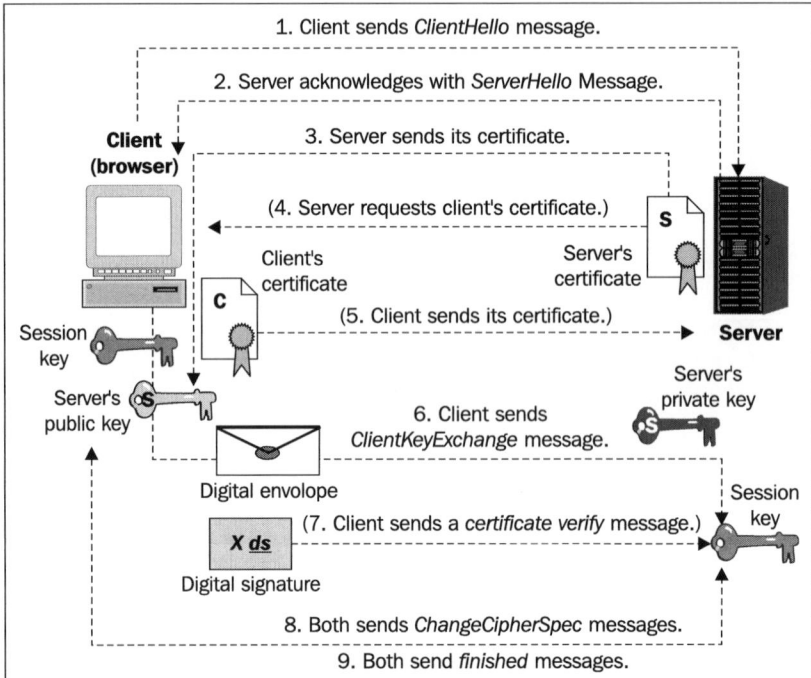

How to do it...

You will need to put the following configuration in your setup and ensure the certificates are in the correct places:

```
mail {
  auth_http  localhost:9000/cgi-bin/auth;

  proxy      on;
  starttls   on; ## enable STARTTLS for all mail servers

  # The config assumes certificates in /etc/nginx/ssl/ and
  # private keys in /etc/nginx/ssl/private/
  ssl                          on;
  ssl_prefer_server_ciphers    on;
  ssl_protocols                TLSv1 SSLv3;
  ssl_ciphers                  HIGH:!ADH:!MD5:@STRENGTH;
  ssl_session_cache            shared:TLSSL:16m;
  ssl_session_timeout          10m;
  ## default SSL cert. Each host should have its own.
  ssl_certificate              ssl/wildcard.crt;
  ssl_certificate_key          ssl/private/wildcard.key;

  ## default, STARTTLS is appended because of starttls directive above
  imap_capabilities "IMAP4rev1"  "UIDPLUS";
  server {
    listen      143;
    protocol    imap;
    server_name  mx.example1.com;
  }

  pop3_capabilities  "TOP"  "USER";
  server {
    listen      110;
    protocol    pop3;
  }
}
```

How it works...

This recipe simply sets up a set of certificates that will be used for every proxy request that comes through Nginx. It uses TLS and SSL, which ensure reliable security based on the browser you have in action.

The other directives help you set the cache sizes and timeout sizes, the defaults are fairly optimal in most use cases and would require tweaking in the event of a significant rise in secure certificate-driven traffic.

Using Nginx as a WEBDAV reverse proxy

Web-based Distributed Authoring and Versioning (WebDAV) is a set of methods based on the Hypertext Transfer Protocol (HTTP) that facilitates collaboration between users in editing and managing documents and files stored on World Wide Web servers. WEBDAV adds more keywords on top of HTTP which support many more keywords, such as PUT, DELETE, MKCOL, COPY, and MOVE.

The WebDAV protocol makes the Web a readable and writable medium. It provides a framework for users to create, change, and move documents on a server (typically a web server or "web share").

This recipe will help us proxy WEBDAV correctly over Nginx. It finds application in SVN over HTTP and many other situations.

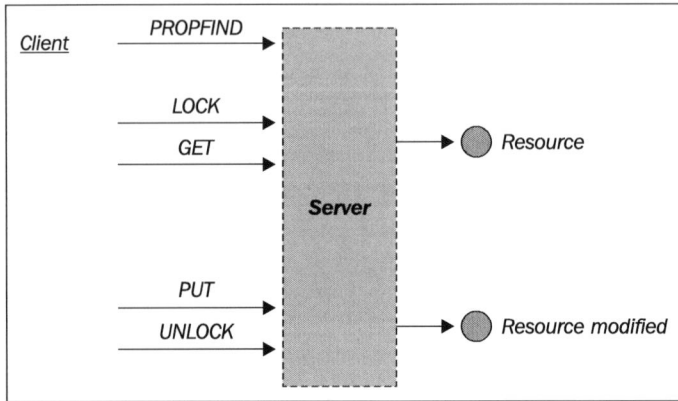

How to do it...

We will first set up the module and then add the configuration necessary for WEBDAV to work properly behind Nginx.

1. We will start with installing the module:

   ```
   ./configure --with-http_dav_module
   make && make install
   ```

2. We will then add configuration in the location directives where we want the WEBDAV supports.

   ```
   root      /data/www/www.example1.com;
   location /files {
      dav_methods  PUT DELETE MKCOL COPY MOVE;
      create_full_put_path    on;
   ```

```
dav_access               group:rw  all:r;
limit_except  GET {
   allow  192.168.1.0/32;
   deny   all;
}
}
```

3. Now we will restart the server to see the changes.

    ```
    /etc/init.d/nginx restart
    ```

How it works...

In this configuration, we set up the various WEBDAV methods that Nginx will support. We then enable the ability to create intermediary directories when a new file is PUT (and the directories above it do not exist). We then use some basic group level permission on which user or group can make the calls and modify the files.

We also put a limit rule that does not allow computers outside the subnet to make anything other than a GET method call. That ensures that someone cannot modify the files maliciously from outside.

Dynamic image resizing using Nginx

Today the Web is about multimedia, and images that form an important part of it. Image resizing, as a result, has become one of the more common web-based tasks. Writing image manipulation code can be tedious and at times, inefficient. To solve this issue, we will have a look at how can one resize images on the fly using Nginx.

How to do it...

So you will need to follow these steps to install the module and then configure Nginx to resize images.

1. You will first need to compile Nginx with this module:

```
./configure -with-http_image_filter_module
Make && make install
```

2. You will then need to add the following configuration in your site configuration:

```
location /img/ {
    proxy_pass      http://backend;
    image_filter    resize   150 100;
    error_page      415   = /empty;
}
location = /empty {
    empty_gif;
}
```

3. You will then need to restart Nginx to complete the installation and configuration.

```
/etc/init.d/nginx restart
```

How it works...

The idea is fairly simple; it acts as an image filter, resizing any image that is uploaded to this endpoint. The directive image_filter takes the resize and size (100 X 100) parameter to do the necessary filtering:

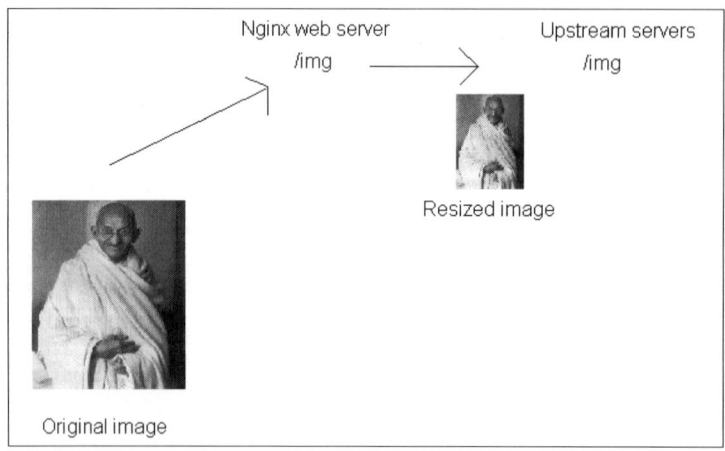

You can set other parameters for the `image_filter` directive and can get it do other forms of image manipulation. The following table lists the possibilities.

Parameter value	Description
test	This checks if the image type is an image format, otherwise it returns an HTTP 415 error code
size	It gives information about the image in the JSON format, for example: `{ "img" : { "width": 100, "height": 100, "type": "gif" } }` If it is not an image it returns `{}`
resize	This proportionally scales the images to the given height and width
Crop	This does not scale, but crops the image to the given height and width

Replacing and searching text in Nginx response

It is sometimes possible that you would need to block or remove certain keywords from the entire site at the shortest notice possible. With much larger sites, and static page sites, this can be a very tedious and time-consuming process. Nginx provides you with a quick way of replacing and searching texts in the response it sends out. In this example, we will clear swear words out of the outputted response.

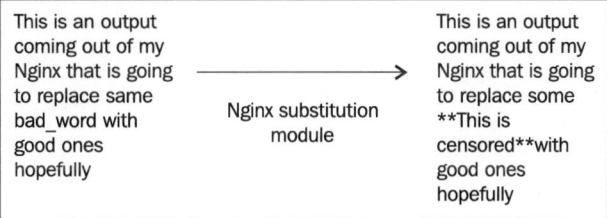

You will first need to install the module, and then we will put in some configuration that will remove all kinds of swear words.

1. You will first compile Nginx with the substitution module.

    ```
    ./configure --with-http_sub_module
    Make && make install
    ```

2. Now we will enter the required configuration to enable the substitution:

```
Server {
Server_name www.example1.com;

...
location / {
  ...
  sub_filter 'bad_word' '**This is censored**';
  sub_filter_once off;
}
}
```

3. We can now safely restart Nginx to complete the installation and see the module in action.

```
/et/init.d/nginx restart
```

How it works...

This piece of configuration basically takes all occurrences of bad_word in the response and substitutes it with '**This is censored**'. The directive sub_filter_once basically ensures that the replacement happens for the first occurrence only; we have switched it off as we want to replace all occurrences.

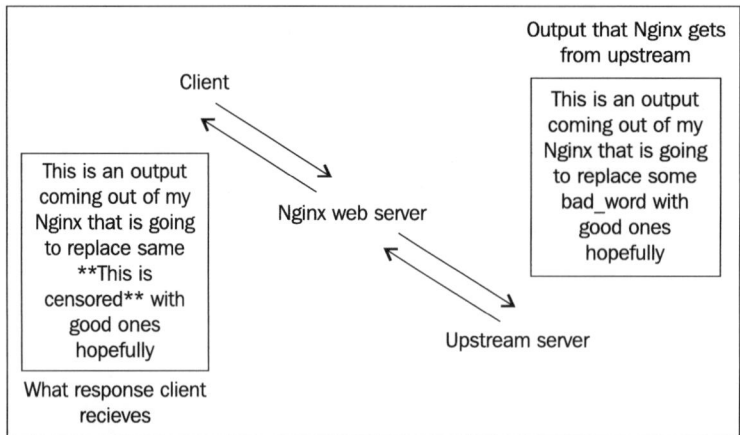

Assembling ZIP files on the fly

An often needed feature on most sites nowadays is the ability to download a compressed version of a file. We will, in this recipe, introduce a module that will take a set of files in the local files system and serve them as a single ZIP file. This is a very efficient module which can easily archive hundreds of megabytes of files.

How to do it...

In this recipe, we will first install the module, and then we will see how it works.

1. You will need to first download the code for the module and then configure Nginx.

    ```
    wget http://wiki.nginx.org/images/6/61/Mod_zip-1.1.6.tar.gz
    tar -xvzf Mod_zip-1.1.6.tar.gz
    cd nginx
    ./configure --add-module=../Mod_zip-1.1.6
    make && make install
    ```

2. You should restart Nginx; the command will differ based on your platform.

    ```
    /etc/init.d/nginx restart
    ```

3. You can then try testing the module by making the following HTTP request. This request should contain "X-Archive-Files: zip" in its header:

    ```
    - 428    /test1.txt    Test file 1.txt
    - 100339 /test2.txt    Test file 2.txt
    ```

4. This should trigger the download of a ZIP archive.

How it works...

The working of this module is interesting, in that we are making a special HTTP request with the "X-Archive-Files: zip" header which triggers this module. What we send is a list of the files that need to be in the archive in the following format:

```
<CRC-32 value> <Filesize in bytes> <file location> <filename in archive>
```

If there is any error in the list of files, then the download is aborted. It is also important to notice in the example that sometimes the CRC-32 value of a file may not be at hand, so you can send "-"in the place of that parameter.

Using Nginx as a HTTP publish-subscribe server

Most of us are using one social network or another, and in recent years it is very clear that the social Internet is all about real-time. Driving this forward is asynchronous JavaScript HTTP calls which come in two forms, the short poll and the long poll.

To explain this let's take the simple example of a real-time updating status page. There are two possible ways of updating this page, one is that the JavaScript periodically fires a request, say every second, and gets an update from the server. This has its pros and cons, as it is clearly not real-time in the true sense. The other approach is the event driven one, where the JavaScript opens a connection with the server and waits till the server responds (which may take quite a while in some cases). The issue with this approach is that this potentially eats up resources for the web server as it waits to send a response to the client. However, due to Nginx's event-driven architecture, it is very cheap for Nginx to keep many connections open concurrently.

In this recipe, we will have a look at an Nginx module that helps you easily implement the HTTP publish-subscribe model using Nginx.

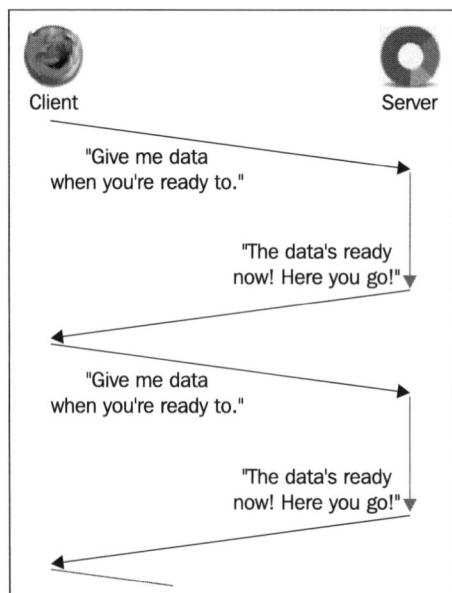

How to do it...

In this recipe we will first install the module and then set up the configuration.

1. We will first download the module and then compile it into Nginx:

    ```
    wget http://pushmodule.slact.net/downloads/nginx_http_push_
    module-0.692.tar.gz

    tar -xvzf nginx_http_push_module-0.692.tar.gz

    cd nginx

    ./configure --add-module=../nginx_http_push_module-0.692

    make && make install
    ```

2. Now the following configuration needs to be inserted in the server directive:

    ```
    # internal publish endpoint (keep it private / protected)
    location /publish {
        set $push_channel_id $arg_id;       #/?id=239aff3 or somesuch
        push_publisher;

        push_store_messages on;             # enable message queueing
        push_message_timeout 2h;            # expire buffered messages
    after 2 hours
        push_max_message_buffer_length 10; # store 10 messages
        push_min_message_recipients 0;      # minimum recipients before
    purge
    }
    # public long-polling endpoint
    location /activity {
        push_subscriber;
        push_subscriber_concurrency broadcast;
        set $push_channel_id $arg_id;
        default_type   text/plain;
    }
    ```

3. We will then restart Nginx.

    ```
    /etc/init.d/nginx restart
    ```

How it works...

This configuration creates a publishing end-point that will take an ID parameter to publish in. It will store the last 10 messages in a buffer for the new recipients who join the channel.

It also creates an activity endpoint, which is actually the long-polling endpoint, which the JavaScript will call and wait for. In its current configuration, it will allow any client who joins the channel to long-poll this end-point. This will make your application dependant on Nginx for the long-poll ability, thus freeing up resources on your application server. Nginx has a lot less overhead for maintaining open connections, which is a necessity in long-poll based activities.

 The preceding site has the TV chatter feed which is driven by the Nginx's publish-subscribe module and scales easily for thousands of users.

There's more...

You can also use this same channel broadcasting mechanism for one-to-one communication as well. So you can set values to the `push_subscriber_concurrency` directive depending on which you can achieve other communication modes.

Modes	Description
last	Only the most recent listener request is kept, 409 for others
first	Only the oldest listener request is kept, 409 for others
broadcast	Any number of listener requests may be long-polling

Transforming XML responses using XSLT templates

Before the advent of JavaScript as the primary client side language, JSON or JavaScript object notation had not really caught on. XML has been the dominant format of exchange for quite some time and most systems continue to support one XML format or another. It is also interesting to note how the newer document formats (new office and open office formats) are also primarily XML standards in a well-packaged archive.

 Nginx gives us the ability to transform the XML responses that it generates into another XML format by the application of a XSLT. This can be very useful in situations where one requires API outputs to fit an external client's requirements without a change to the end-point.

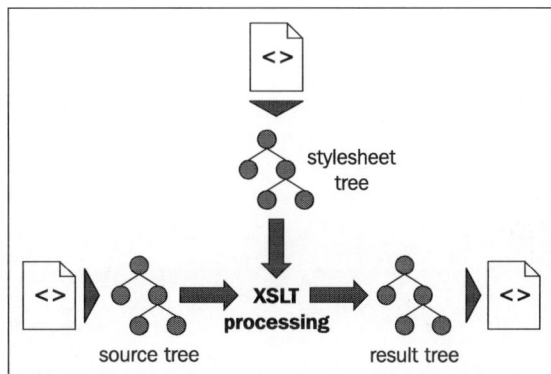

How to do it...

We will first install the module and then configure your site setup.

1. You will need to install the XSL module:

   ```
   ./configure --with-http_xslt_module
   make && make install
   ```

2. Insert the following configuration into your server directive:

   ```
   server {
   server_name www.example1.com;
   . . .
   location / {
     . . .
   }
   location /xml_api {
   ```

```
        xml_entities        /site/dtd/entities.dtd;
        xslt_stylesheet     /site/xslt/one.xslt    param1="value";
        . . .
    }
}
```

3. Restart Nginx.

```
/etc/init.d/nginx restart
```

How it works...

This configuration allows you to apply one XSLT transform on all the XML responses that the `/xml_api` endpoint generates. This also allows you to set parameters in the XSLT based on your Nginx variables (or GET parameters).

Setting up Etags for static content

Etags are a part of the HTTP protocol and is utilized for cache validation. This allows more efficiency on the part of the web browser and saves bandwidth as well. You can think of Etags as Unique IDs which represent the current state of a URL.

Nginx does not generate Etags for the static content that it serves, and as a result you are not able to make full use of the advantages of Etags. In this recipe, we will install a module that will get your static content running with Etags in a jiffy.

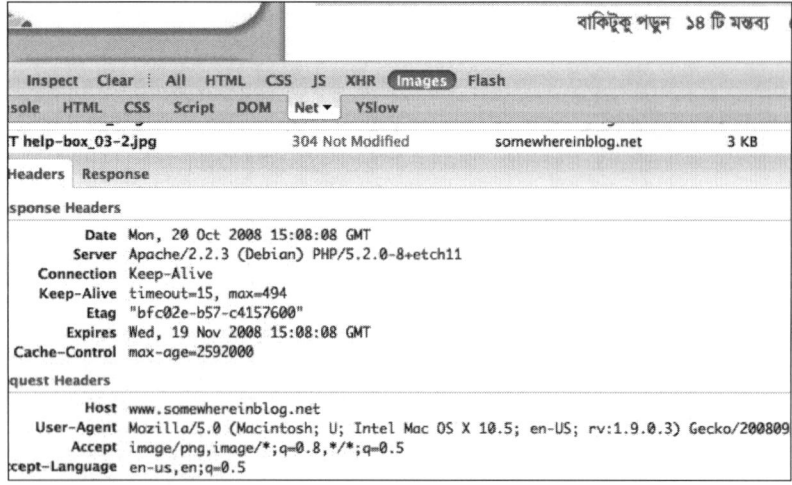

How to do it...

1. We will first install the module:

```
git clone git://github.com/mikewest/nginx-static-etags.git ./
nginx-static-etags

cd nginx

./configure --add-module=../nginx-static-etags

make && make install
```

2. Now we can place the following directives in the locations where we want the static files to contain the Etags directive:

```
location / {

    ...

    FileETag on;

    ...

}
```

3. You need to restart Nginx to see the affect.

```
/etc/init.d/nginx restart
```

How it works...

This directive basically adds the ability for Nginx to have a look at the static files being served and add an ETag to the HTTP header. When the files change, the Etag header changes accordingly, this ensures cache invalidation on the client's browser and downloading of the new updated static file.

Easy logging of page load times

If you are in the business of running portals or websites, the speed of your site is one of the most important parts of your interaction with the end user. You would want to find out the slower parts of your website and possibly optimize your codebase to respond to those requests faster.

This recipe has a look at a module that helps you log the page load times and then you can parse those logs to find out the part of the sites that take the most amount of time to load up.

How to do it...

This recipe involves the setting up of the module and then a re-configuration of the logging format to output the page load time variable. We also run a parser to get a list of the slower pages on the site.

1. We will need to install this module first:

```
wget http://wiki.nginx.org/images/7/78/Ngx_http_log_request_speed.
tar.gz
tar -xvzf Ngx_http_log_request_speed.tar.gz
cd nginx
./configure --add-module=../Ngx_http_log_request_speed
make && make install
```

2. We will configure Nginx to log the page loading times as well:

```
user         www www;
worker_processes   2;
error_log   logs/error.log;
pid          logs/nginx.pid;
events {
        worker_connections  1024;
}
http {
        log_request_speed_filter on;
        log_request_speed_filter_timeout 3;
        . . .

}
```

3. Now we need to restart Nginx.

```
/etc/init.d/nginx restart
```

4. Run the site for some time, and then you can run the log parser to see some analysis:

```
wget http://wiki.nginx.org/images/a/a8/Log_Analyzer.tar.gz
cd Log_Analyzer
tail -n 10000 /var/log/nginx/error.log  | grep 'process request' |
./analyzer.pl  -r
POST /message/ajaxWrite/from_profile/toni32 HTTP/1.1 --- avg ms:
3110, value count: 1
POST /sessionupdate_prod.php HTTP/1.1 --- avg ms: 3312, value
count: 137
GET /favoriten/1 HTTP/1.1 --- avg ms: 3345, value count: 76
GET /nachrichten/read/in/neu/369217567 HTTP/1.1 --- avg ms: 3737,
value count: 1
POST /login_prod.php HTTP/1.1 --- avg ms: 4117, value count: 14
GET /wan/isonline?NICKNAME=luckynight&rtime=1259292758 HTTP/1.1
--- avg ms: 5267, value count: 1
GET /sessionupdate_prod.php HTTP/1.1 --- avg ms: 5572, value
count: 8
```

How it works...

In the preceding steps we have installed the plugin which adds a Nginx variable that keeps track of the amount of time the backend takes to respond. This variable can now be easily logged, giving you performance insights without writing extra code. After logging, you can use a simple script for this extra column to find out the slower pages.

The directive `log_request_speed_filter_timeout` basically sets a cut-off of three seconds, above which all pages will be logged. This prevents unnecessary time logging of pages.

Streaming of MP4/H.264 files

Video streaming has become a social phenomenon with the rise of sites such as YouTube (`http://youtube.com`), Metacafe (`http://metacafe.com`), and Dailymotion (`http://dailymotion.com`). Most of these sites either stream FLV files or MP4 files. We have covered how you can efficiently stream FLV files and now we will cover MP4.

Nginx supports an MP4 streaming module that allows you to easily stream and seek MP4 files.

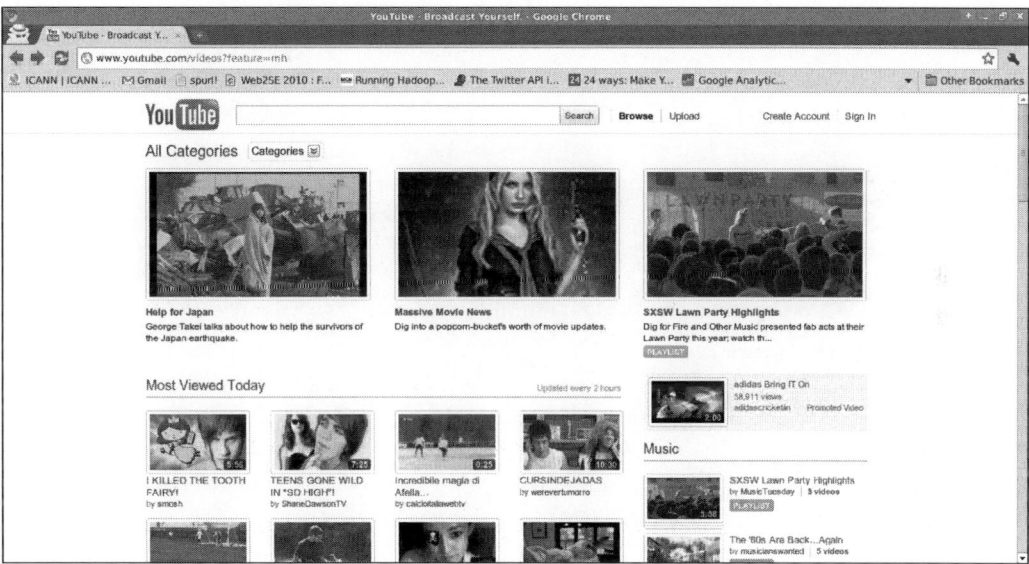

How to do it...

In this recipe, we will first install the module and then configure a particular location to serve the MP4 video files.

1. We will first install the module:

```
wget http://i.6.cn/nginx_mp4_streaming_public_20081229.tar.bz2
tar -xvjf nginx_mp4_streaming_public_20081229.tar.bz2
cd nginx
./configure --add-module=../nginx_mp4_streaming_public_20081229
make && make install
```

2. Now we will add the following configuration to the location directive where your video files reside:

```
server {
server_name www.example1.com;
. . .
root /var/www/www.example1.com;
location / {
. . .
}
location /videos {
mp4;
. . .
}
}
```

3. We will need to restart Nginx to apply the settings.

```
/etc/init.d/nginx restart
```

How it works...

All you require to support MP4 files streaming is to add the directive above. This module ensures that you can seek to random parts of the file as well.

Setting up SCGI sites

Nginx supports SCGI out of the box, and as a result it is rather straightforward to set up. This is supposed to be an alternative to CGI, much like FastCGI. In this recipe, we will assume that you already have an SCGI backend and we will go ahead and set up Nginx as the frontend proxy server.

FastCGI has a fairly complicated protocol, as compared to SCGI which makes it prone to efficiency issues. Due to the simplicity of the protocol definition which is 100 lines long (`http://python.ca/nas/scgi/protocol.txt`), SCGI is considered and often found to be a faster and more efficient CGI replacement as compared to FastCGI.

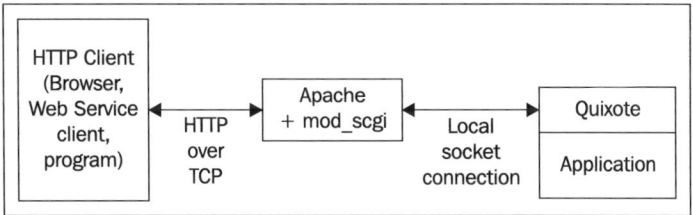

How to do it...

To get this running, all you need to do is to use the following configuration in your setup and then restart Nginx:

```
http {
  scgi_cache_path    /usr/local/nginx/temp  levels=1:2
                     keys_zone=NAME:10m
                     inactive=5m;

  server {
    location / {
      scgi_pass    127.0.0.1:9000;
      scgi_cache    NAME;
      scgi_cache_valid    200 302  1h;
      scgi_cache_valid    301      1d;
      scgi_cache_valid    any      1m;
      scgi_cache_min_uses  1;
      scgi_cache_use_stale error  timeout invalid_header http_500;
    }
  }
}
```

How it works...

This assumes that you have an SCGI backend running on localhost on port 9000. This configuration sets up an SCGI cache of 10MBs which caches all 2000K files for a minute. This is very similar to how the FastCGI cache works.

Setting up expiring links

A lot of the time, security comes as a factor of time limits and obfuscation. We will explore a module here which will let you generate links that are valid until a certain Date/Time.

How to do it...

We will set up the module and then setup the secure download location.

1. We will first install the module:

   ```
   git clone https://github.com/replay/ngx_http_secure_download.git
   cd nginx
   ./configure --add-module=../ngx_http_secure_download
   make && make install
   ```

2. We will need to add the following configuration under the server directive:

   ```
   location /timedfolder {
               secure_download on;
               secure_download_secret IAmSalt$remote_addr;
               secure_download_path_mode file;
               if ($secure_download = "-1") {
                   rewrite /expired.html break;
               }
               if ($secure_download = "-2") {
                   rewrite /bad_hash.html break;
               }
               if ($secure_download = "-3") {
                   return 500;
               }
               rewrite ^(.*)/[0-9a-zA-Z]*/[0-9a-zA-Z]*$ $1 break;
   }
   ```

3. We will need to restart Nginx for the configurations to apply.

   ```
   /etc/init.d/nginx restart
   ```

How it works...

In this configuration, we have enabled the module and set the md5 secret as IAmSalt$remote_addr. The path mode is file which means that the hash created contains the file name. The URL generated has the following structure:

```
<real_path>/<md5_hash>/<expiration_timestamp>
```

The md5 hash gets generated out of the following string:

`<real_path>/<secret>/<expiration_timestamp>`

- ▶ `real_path` can be either the path of the file which you want to access or the folder which contains the file
- ▶ `secret` is the hash defined
- ▶ `expiration_timestamp` is a unix_timestamp (seconds since beginning of 1970) in hexadecimal format

So an example URL would be like the one below:

`http://www.example1.com/timefolder/protected.html/f901b5272c17b456fab f49c3e9bcc120/49F71056`

10
Some More Third-party Modules

In this chapter, we will cover:

- ▶ Configuring a fair load balancing
- ▶ Setting up health checks for backend servers
- ▶ Tracking and reporting file upload progress
- ▶ Generating circles for round edges using Nginx
- ▶ Running Python using Phusion Passenger
- ▶ Generating graphs directly from RRDtool in Nginx
- ▶ Using Google performance tools
- ▶ Serving content directly from GridFS
- ▶ Configuring Basic HTTP auth using PAM
- ▶ Configuring Basic HTTP auth using Kerberos

Introduction

This chapter looks at various web situations such as load balancing, server health checks, and more which will be very useful in a production environment. These simple recipes will be highly applicable in enterprise scenarios where you may need to have analytics, external authentication schemes, and many other situations.

Configuring a fair load balancing

Nginx by default uses a round robin mechanism to proxy requests to its backend servers. Most of the time this is sufficient, as the machines on the backend are usually of the same build and configuration, but in many cases it necessary to implement a fair load. This balance takes into account the existing load on a machine before its proxies the requests. This is where the Nginx fair scheduler plugin comes in. It enables the system administrator to configure fair scheduling and allows the backend machines to be of dissimilar performance, and yet the whole system will perform optimally.

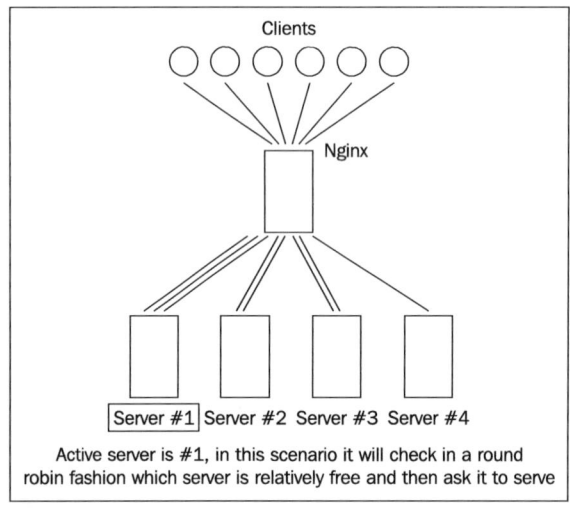

How to do it...

We will first download the plugin, install it, and then configure it in the steps described ahead.

1. We will first install the fair scheduling module:

   ```
   git clone git://github.com/gnosek/nginx-upstream-fair.git
   cd nginx
   ./configure --add-module=../nginx-upstream-fair
   make
   make install
   ```

2. We will then put the following in our Nginx configuration:

   ```
   upstream backend {
       server 192.168.1.3;
       server 192.168.1.5;
       fair;
   ```

```
        }
        server {
                server_name www.example1.com;
                ...
                location / {
                        proxy_pass http://backend;
                        ...
                }
        }
```

3. Now, we need to restart Nginx to see the changes:

    /etc/init.d/nginx restart

How it works...

This module lets you configure a weighted least connection round robin mechanism, which keeps track of the real-time load on each individual backend server to make a decision on whom to proxy it to.

The module also allows you to track the load on each server by visiting a web page; this can be easily integrated into your web infrastructure monitoring systems.

There's more...

We can also configure the module to handle the following scheduling cases:

Modes	Description
Default	This lets us configure the simple weighted least-connection round robin, which basically means you give the request to the server with the least active connections in a round-robin fashion. This is the default mode explained in the preceding example.
no_rr	This disables round robin, which would be applicable in cases where we may be spawning multiple backends depending on your load. It will ensure that Nginx uses as many backends as it needs.
weight_mode=idle no_rr	This mode attempts to balance the load between the minimum pool of backend servers. It can help us identify the actual number of backend servers.
weight_mode=peak	In this mode, Nginx will not send requests to the backend beyond a certain limit. If all the backends are full the client will receive a 502 error.

The following diagram shows a scenario how servers respond when they are busy:

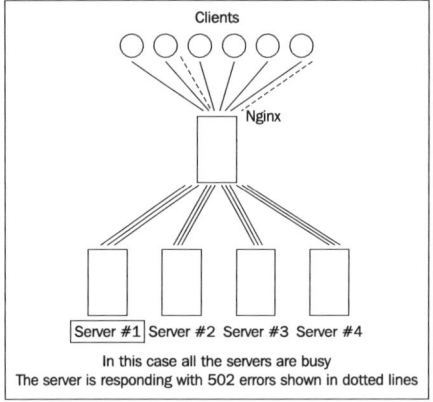

See also

Chapter 7, Setup load balancing with reverse proxy

Setting up health checks for backend servers

One of the most important aspects of running a fairly large Internet site is the ability to understand the health of your machines. In huge server farms, it is not physically possible to inspect the health of the machines one by one, or for that matter to detect which backend server is down.

To solve this problem, Nginx has a neat module which will let you run a regular check on all the backend servers and mark them as bad when they do not behave accordingly. Marking them as bad ensures that the end client's request never gets sent to the backend server with issues by Nginx. There are very little performance overheads as Nginx maintains all the health check numbers in memory.

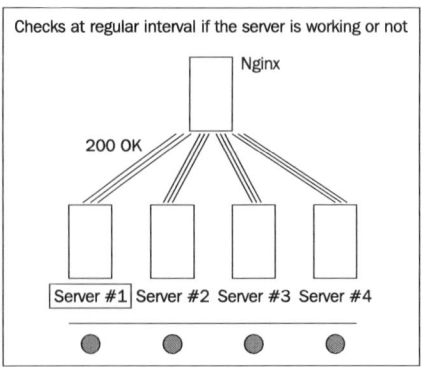

How to do it...

1. We will first install the Nginx backend health module:

```
git clone https://github.com/cep21/healthcheck_nginx_upstreams.git
cd nginx
./configure --add-module=../ healthcheck_nginx_upstreams
make
make install
```

2. We will then put the following in the configuration files:

```
upstream backend {
    server 192.168.1.2;
    server 192.168.1.5;
    healthcheck_enabled;
    healthcheck_delay 60000;
}
server {
        server_name www.example1.com;
        ...
        location / {
                proxy_pass http://backend;
                ...
        }
        location /backend_status {
                healthcheck_status;
        }
}
```

3. Now, restart Nginx to see the changes.

```
/etc/init.d/nginx restart
```

How it works...

This module makes a query to the backend servers every minute and then updates the status of every backend server. This was achieved with the healthcheck_enabled and healthcheck_delay directives.

We have enabled the health check status page as well, so we can check out the status of the backend server by visiting `http://www.example1.com/backend_status`.

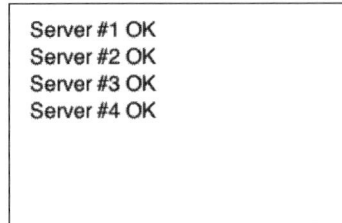

```
Server #1 OK
Server #2 OK
Server #3 OK
Server #4 OK
```

Tracking and reporting file upload progress

File uploading is one of the most common activities on a website. It is achieved by making a multi-part POST submission, which does not allow you to track the progress of the file upload. So if your user is uploading a fairly large file, he expects to be notified about the speed of upload and the time it will take. To ensure that the user is aware, there is a module that helps us track how far the file has been uploaded to the server.

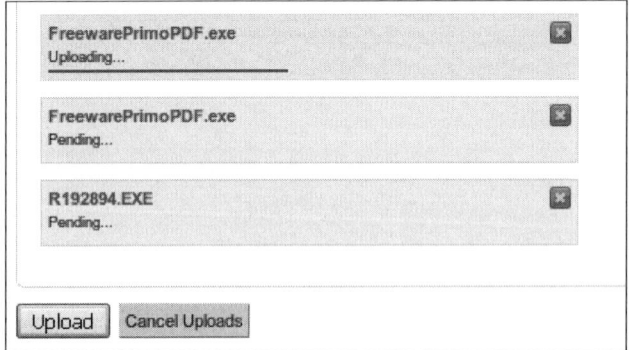

How to do it...

We will first install the plugin, and then see how to configure it in the following steps.

1. We will first install the Nginx file upload progress module:

```
git clone https://github.com/masterzen/nginx-upload-progress-
module.git
cd nginx./configure --add-module=../nginx-upload-progress-module
make
make install
```

2. We will use the following in our Nginx configuration:

```
http {
    upload_progress proxied 1m;
  server {
        server_name   www.example1.com;
        root /var/www/www.example1.com;
        location / {
            proxy_pass http://127.0.0.1;
            proxy_redirect default;
            track_uploads proxied 30s;
        }
        location ^~ /progress {
            report_uploads proxied;
        }
    }
}
```

3. A restart of Nginx will apply those changes:

```
/etc/init.d/nginx restart
```

How it works...

This configuration basically sets up a 1MB cache to keep track of the uploaded file status. Every file uploaded should be assigned a tracking ID, using which one can query http:// www.example1.com/progress to find out how much of the file has uploaded till now. It can return a lot of formats based on how we have configured the module output; in this example it will output JSON by default.

It is important to note that to track the file progress we will need to append an X-Progress-ID, which will uniquely identify the file being uploaded.

Generating circles for round edges using Nginx

The latest in Internet aesthetics are rounded edges, and clearly Nginx is not going to be left behind. This recipe has a look at an interesting module that allows you to generate dynamic circles, which we can easily utilize for creating round edge styles. This is most applicable when you need to support rounded edges on older browsers that are not compatible with CSS3.

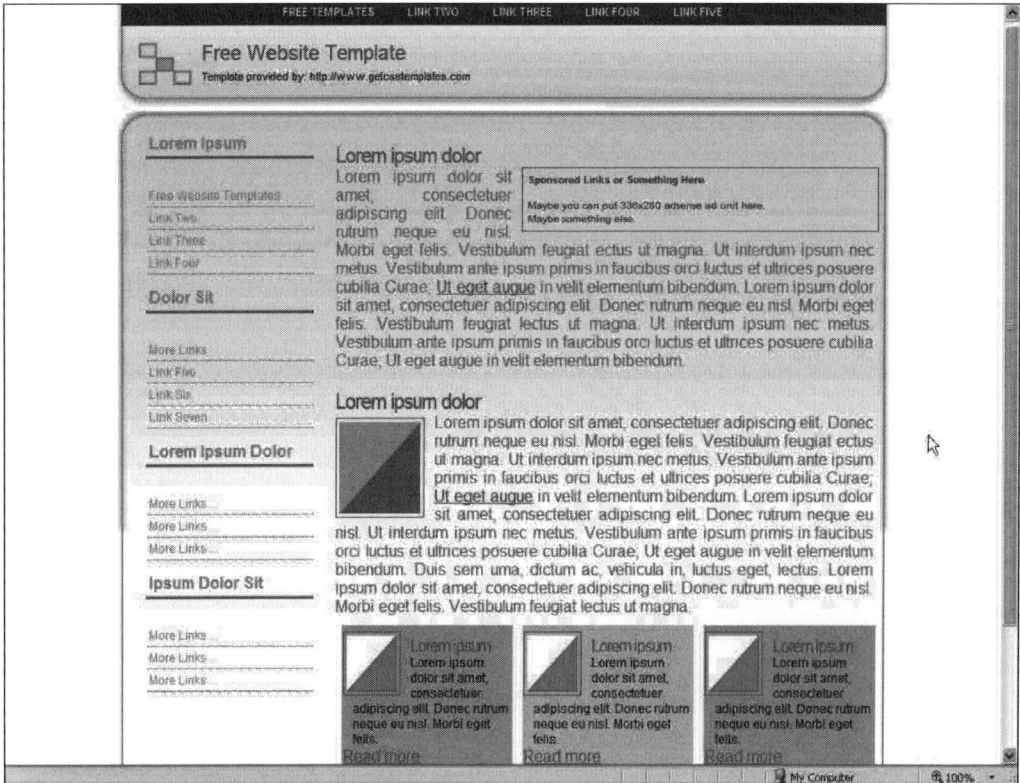

How to do it...

We will first install the plugin and then configure it in the following steps.

1. We will first need to install the Nginx Circle GIF module:

   ```
   wget http://wiki.nginx.org/images/b/b6/Nginx_circle_gif-
   0.1.3.tar.gz

   tar -xvzf Nginx_circle_gif-0.1.3.tar.gz

   cd nginx
   ```

```
./configure –add-module=../ Nginx_circle_gif-0.1.3

make

make install
```

2. We will then use the following in our Nginx configuration:

```
server {
        server_name www.example1.com;
        ...
        location / {
                proxy_pass http://backend;
                ...
        }
        location /circle {
                circle_gif;
        }
}
```

3. Now, restart Nginx to see the changes.

```
/etc/init.d/nginx restart
```

How it works...

Configuring this module is simply adding a new URL endpoint, which will act as a web API to generate the gif. The format of the URL is as follows:

```
<background color>/<foreground color>/<radius>.gif
```

So the following URL will generate a black on white circle of radius 10 pixels. We can use this to generate the rounded corner styles:

```
http://www.example1.com/circles/ffffff/000000/10.gif
```

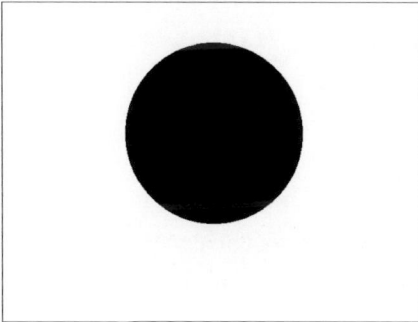

Running Python using Phusion Passenger

Nginx's primary purpose, to act as a state-of-art web and mail proxy server, has curtailed its image as that of an all-purpose server, of which it is fully capable. We will have a look at how can we run Python applications with Phusion Passenger as the backend.

How to do it...

We will first install all the dependencies required to install Phusion Passenger and then configure Nginx with it in the following steps.

1. We will first install Ruby:

   ```
   apt-get update
   apt-get -y install build-essential zlib1g zlib1g-dev libxml2
   libxml2-dev libxslt-dev
   wget http://ftp.ruby-lang.org/pub/ruby/1.9/ruby-1.9.2-p0.tar.gz
   tar -xvf ruby-1.9.2-p0.tar.gz
   ./configuremake
   make install
   ```

2. We need to install `rubygems`, which is the package management tool for Ruby:

   ```
   wget http://rubyforge.org/frs/download.php/60718/rubygems-
   1.3.5.tgz
   tar zxvf ./rubygems-1.3.5.tgz
   cd rubygems-1.3.5
   sudo ruby setup.rb
   ```

3. We will install rails and Passenger Phusion:

   ```
   gem install rails
   gem install passenger
   ```

4. We will install the Passenger Phusion Nginx module, as shown in the following screenshot:

Passenger-install-nginx-module

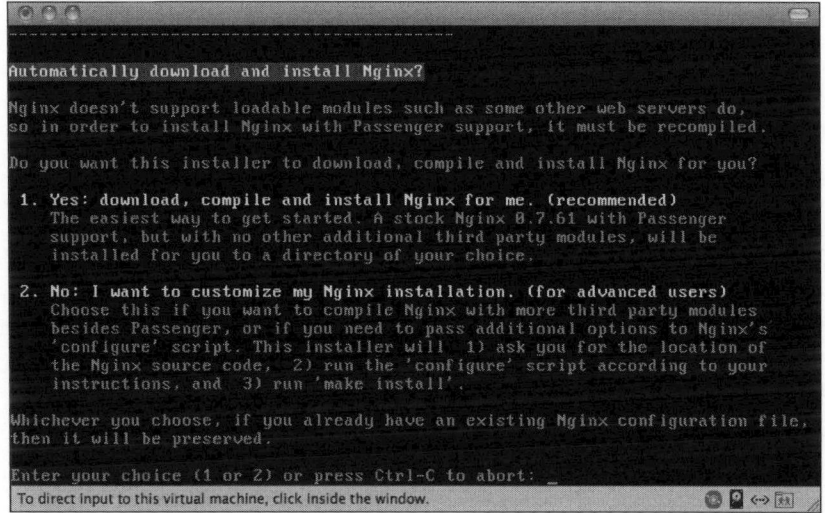

5. The following configuration is used in nginx.conf and it assumes that the application is placed at /var/www/www.example1.com/.

```
worker_processes  1;
events {
    worker_connections  1024;
}
http {
 include        mime.types;
    default_type  application/octet-stream;

    sendfile        on;     keepalive_timeout   65;
        gzip  on;
    passenger_root /usr/local/lib/ruby/gems/1.9.1/gems/
passenger-2.2.5;     passenger_ruby /usr/local/bin/ruby;

    server {
        listen        80;
        server_name  localhost;
                root /opt/nginx/html/public/;
                passenger_enabled on
}
}
```

6. Now, a Nginx restart should let you see all the changes at work.

```
/etc/init.d/nginx restart
```

How it works...

Phusion Passenger is a very easy way to deploy production application in Rails, which is a web framework in Ruby. It is also very efficient at deploying Python (WSGI) applications. In this recipe, we have gone ahead and set up a small Python web script to demonstrate this capability.

See also

Chapter 6, Setting up a Python site using uWSGI

Generating graphs directly from RRDtool in Nginx

A lot of sites today show analytics as a part of their offering. The most common form of analytics representation is the time-based graphs, which are very efficiently generated by RRDtool, which is a really good open source graph generation tool. In this recipe, we will explore a module that will create a web API that you can dynamically call to get your graphs.

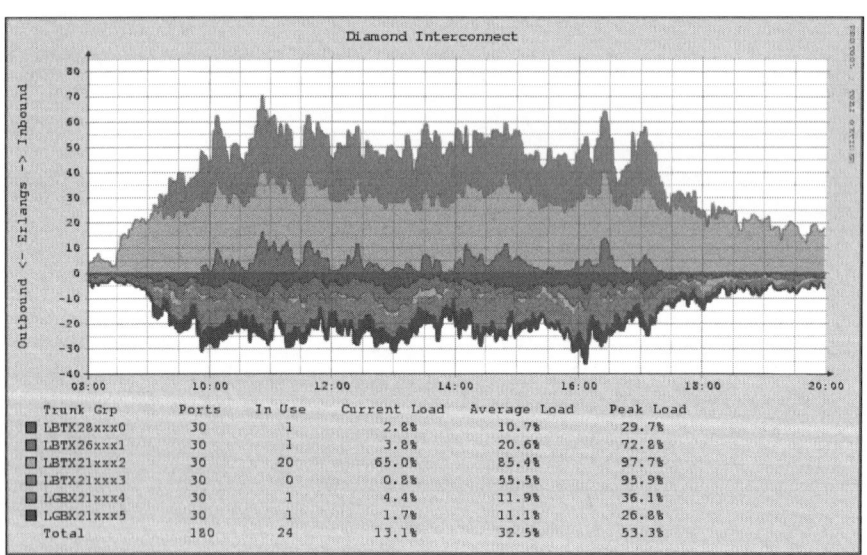

How to do it...

We will first install the plugin and then configure it in the following steps.

1. We will install the Nginx RRDtool module; it assumes that you have already installed RRDtools:

   ```
   wget http://wiki.nginx.org/images/9/9d/Mod_rrd_graph-0.2.0.tar.gz
   tar -xvzf Mod_rrd_graph-0.2.0.tar.gz
   cd nginx
   ./configure -add-module=../Mod_rrd_graph-0.2.0
   make
   make install
   ```

2. We will then use the following in our configuration:

   ```
   server {
           server_name www.example1.com;
           ...
           location / {

             ...
           }
           location /rrd_gen {
                   rrd_graph;
           }
   }
   ```

3. Now, restart Nginx to see the changes.

   ```
   /etc/init.d/nginx restart
   ```

How it works...

This set up is easy to demonstrate. Let's say that we want to generate a graph using the following set of commands in the RRDtool:

```
rrdtool graph --start now-300s \--end now \
DEF:ds0=test.rrd:reading:AVERAGE \
LINE1:ds0#00FF00
```

You can generate the following URL, which will return the preceding graph, but it will appear as a web URL which will simplify your life drastically. This URL contains the preceding code in an URL encoded format appended to the `http://www.example1.com/rrd_gen` URL.

```
http://www.example1.com/rrd_gen--start%20now-300s%20--end%20now%20
DEF%3Ads0%3Dtest.rrd%3Areading%3AAVERAGE%20LINE1%3Ads0%2300FF00
```

Using Google performance tools

The more experienced Nginx user may actually need to look into limitations of the Nginx platform, in those cases libraries such as Google performance tools make life very easy for the developers. We will look at setting up the Google performance tools module in this recipe.

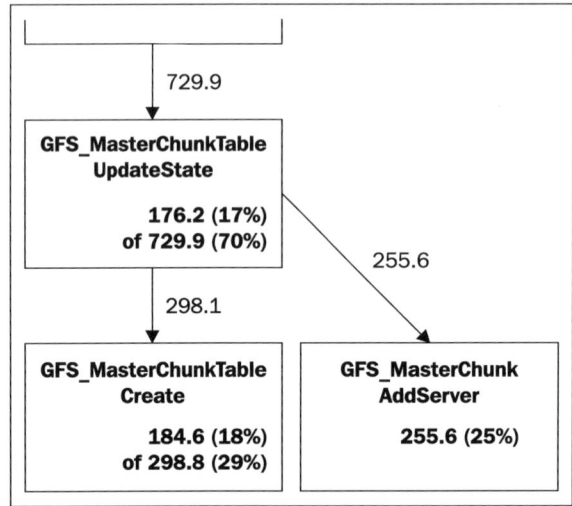

How to do it...

We will first install the plugin and then configure it in the following steps.

1. We will first install the Google performance Nginx module:

   ```
   cd nginx
   ./configure --with-google_perftools_module
   make
   make install
   ```

2. Use the following in your configuration:

   ```
   worker_processes  1;
   events {
       worker_connections  1024;
   }
   google_perftools_profiles log/profile;
   http {
       include       mime.types;
       default_type  application/octet-stream;
   ```

```
sendfile          on;
keepalive_timeout  65;
    gzip  on;
.  .  .
```

3. We will need to restart Nginx to see the changes.

   /etc/init.d/nginx restart

How it works...

This simple directive will let us profile our worker threads. The generated profile files are defined by the `google_perftools_profiles` directive, and this configuration will generate files such as `log/profile.<pid>` where `pid` is the process ID of the worker thread whose profiling information it is.

Serving content directly from GridFS

GridFS is a specification for storing large files in MongoDB. It basically aims to split down files into smaller chunks which are easily manageable, and allows efficient range operations. We will have a look at how we can configure Nginx to serve content directly from GridFS, thereby creating a situation where you can manage all your large files through GridFS and serve them using Nginx.

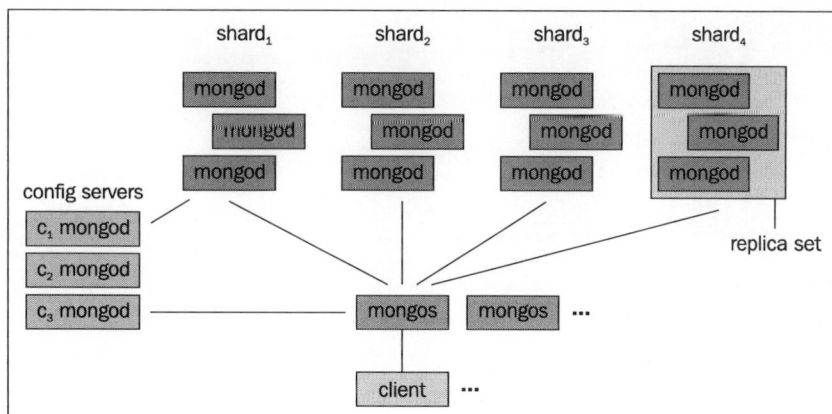

How to do it...

We will first install the plugin and then configure Nginx in the following steps.

1. This recipe assumes that you have installed GridFS. We will install the Nginx gridFS module:

   ```
   git clone https://github.com/mdirolf/nginx-gridfs.git
   cd nginx-gridfs
   git submodule init
   git submodule update
   cd ../nginx
   ./configure --add-module=../nginx-gridfs
   make
   make install
   ```

2. We will put the following in our Nginx configuration:

   ```
   server {
   listen 80;
   server_name www.example1.com;
   . . .
   location /gridfs/ {
       gridfs my_app
               root_collection=pics
               field=_id
               type=int
               user=foo
               pass=bar;
       mongo 127.0.0.1:27017;
   }
   }
   ```

3. Now, restart Nginx to check out the changes. Do make sure that GridFS is running before you test.

   ```
   /etc/init.d/nginx restart
   ```

How it works...

The configuration above enables the GridFS on a MongoDB database called my_app, with the username password as foo and bar respectively. Any call made like http://www.example1.com/gridfs/123/ will return the corresponding file from the *pic* collection with the ID 123.

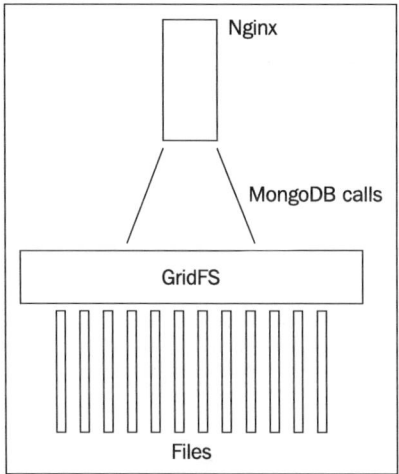

Configuring Basic HTTP auth using PAM

Nginx supports HTTP authentication, and as we have seen in earlier recipes, we can generate `htpasswd` files which contain the valid username and passwords. However, most systems have an existing authentication system that already integrates with PAM, and Nginx has a plugin that already lets you authenticate with PAM.

[PAM is a mechanism that integrates low-level authentication schemes into high level programming API, thus all your programs can operate independently to how your login system operates.]

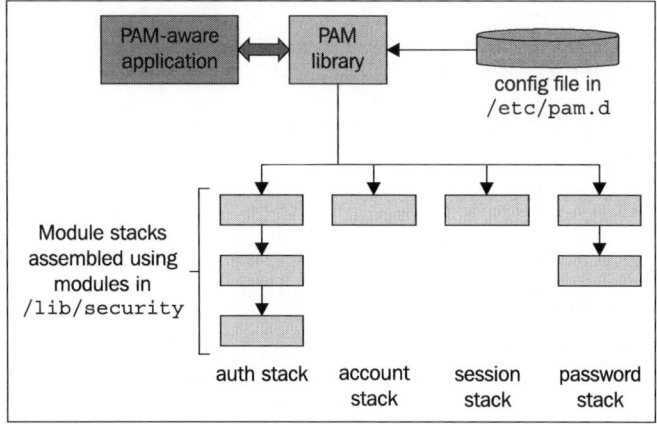

The recipe describes a situation where you want to protect `http://www.example1.com/` `downloads` and ensure that only LDAP authenticated users can access that part of the site.

How to do it...

We will first install the PAM authentication model and then configure Nginx in the following steps.

1. We will first install the Nginx PAM auth module. This recipe assumes that you have an already configured and working LDAP setup.

    wget `http://web.iti.upv.es/~sto/nginx/ngx_http_auth_pam_module-` `1.2.tar.gz`

    tar -xvzf ngx_http_auth_pam_module-1.2.tar.gz

    cd nginx

    ./configure –add-module=../ngx_http_auth_pam_module-1.2

    make

    make install

2. We will then put the following in our Nginx configuration:

    ```
    server {
    server_name www.example1.com;
    . . .
    location /downloads {
        auth_pam          "Downloads";
        auth_pam_service_name "nginx";
    }
    }
    ```

3. We will need to put the following in `/etc/pam.d/nginx`:

    ```
    auth     required     /lib/security/pam_ldap.so
    account  required     /lib/security/pam_ldap.so
    ```

4. Now, you will need to restart your Nginx server.

    /etc/init.d/nginx restart

How it works...

This module basically utilizes PAM as the top level API to access the LDAP authentication structures. It first enables the authentication in the necessary location, which is `/downloads` in this case. Then we set up a PAM service called Nginx, that basically utilizes the PAM LDAP libraries to complete the authentication.

Configuring Basic HTTP auth using Kerberos

If you are using Windows based systems in a heterogeneous environment, in all probability you must use Kerberos as your authentication protocol. In situations where we are deploying a site internally it may be useful to handle web authentication with Kerberos. Nginx has the solution for this, as it has a module that lets you authenticate the user using Kerberos.

This recipe will take a look at how you can protect a particular web location using HTTP authentication using Kerberos as the backend. This is a highly experimental plugin, and only useful when you do not have an alternative to this form of authentication in your network.

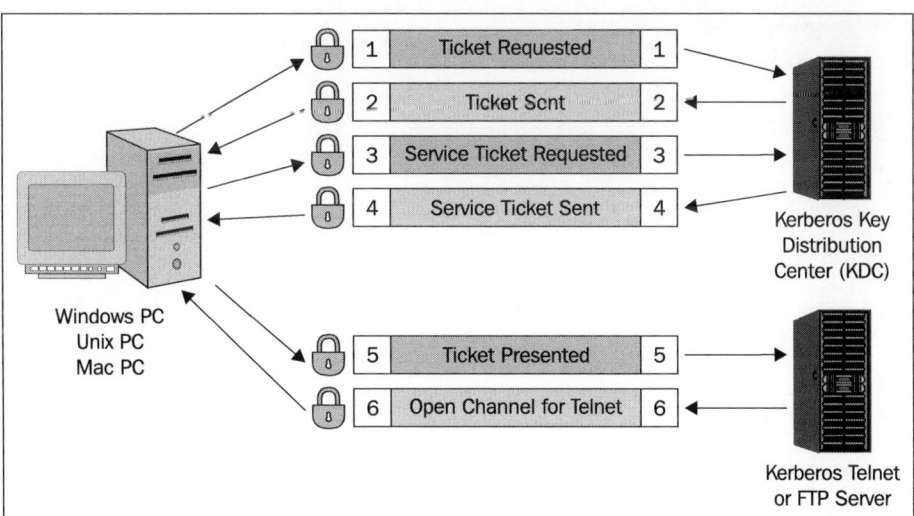

How to do it...

In this recipe, we first install the plugin and then configure Nginx to use it in the following steps.

1. We will first install the Nginx Kerberos module:

   ```
   git clone https://github.com/mike503/spnego-http-auth-nginx-
   module.git

   cd nginx

   ./configure –add-module=../spnego-http-auth-nginx-module

   make

   make install
   ```

2. Now we will configure the module:

   ```
   location /downloads {
       auth_gss on;
       auth_gss_realm LOCALDOMAIN;
       auth_gss_keytab /etc/krb5.keytab;
       auth_gss_service_name HTTP;
   }
   ```

3. Restart Nginx for the changes to take effect.

   ```
   /etc/init.d/nginx restart
   ```

How it works...

This module defines the realm name, and then we will need to define the location of the service credentials. Finally, we set up the service that you use to acquire the credentials.

There are some assumptions that the preceding configuration makes. Your Nginx web server should be in the same broadcast scope of the Kerberos server and so should the client, who will be authenticated to that server.

In another scenario, it is possible that you already have PAM with Kerberos support set up on your server. In this case you can use the preceding recipe to set up PAM with Kerberos.

See also

The *Configuring basic HTTP auth using PAM* recipe, in this chapter

Index

V

valid flag 72
vanilla installation 9
variables
  using, in rewrites 37
Verisign Inc 98
video 162
video streaming 185
virtual hosts
  access logs, creating for 72, 73
  error logs, creating for 72, 73
  wildcards, using in 18

W

Web 173
webalizer 68, 76
Web-based Distributed Authoring and
    Versioning. *See* WebDAV
WebDAV 166, 172
WEBDAV reverse proxy
  Nginx, using as 172, 173
web page encoding
  modifying 30
web server 172
Web Server Gateway Interface. *See* WSGI
weight_mode=idle no_rr 193
weight_mode=peak 193
white space
  removing, from responses 145
wilcards
  using, in virtual hosts 18
wildcard certificates
  using, with multiple servers 101-103

WINCH signal 11

WordPress
  about 46
  configuring 106
WordPress site
  setting up, with static file serving 47-50
worker_connections directive 19
worker_processes configuration 12, 19
wp-supercache plugin 50
WSGI 105, 106, 110
www domain
  redirecting, to non-www domain for
      SEO 144, 145

X

XML responses
  transforming, XSLT templates used 181, 182
XSLT templates
  XML responses, transforming with 181, 182
XSLT transformation 166

Y

Yahoo! 143
yahoobot 87
YouTube
  URL 162, 185

Z

ZIP files
  assembling 176, 177

Thank you for buying
Nginx 1 Web Server Implementation Cookbook

About Packt Publishing

Packt, pronounced 'packed', published its first book "*Mastering phpMyAdmin for Effective MySQL Management*" in April 2004 and subsequently continued to specialize in publishing highly focused books on specific technologies and solutions.

Our books and publications share the experiences of your fellow IT professionals in adapting and customizing today's systems, applications, and frameworks. Our solution based books give you the knowledge and power to customize the software and technologies you're using to get the job done. Packt books are more specific and less general than the IT books you have seen in the past. Our unique business model allows us to bring you more focused information, giving you more of what you need to know, and less of what you don't.

Packt is a modern, yet unique publishing company, which focuses on producing quality, cutting-edge books for communities of developers, administrators, and newbies alike. For more information, please visit our website: www.packtpub.com.

About Packt Open Source

In 2010, Packt launched two new brands, Packt Open Source and Packt Enterprise, in order to continue its focus on specialization. This book is part of the Packt Open Source brand, home to books published on software built around Open Source licences, and offering information to anybody from advanced developers to budding web designers. The Open Source brand also runs Packt's Open Source Royalty Scheme, by which Packt gives a royalty to each Open Source project about whose software a book is sold.

Writing for Packt

We welcome all inquiries from people who are interested in authoring. Book proposals should be sent to author@packtpub.com. If your book idea is still at an early stage and you would like to discuss it first before writing a formal book proposal, contact us; one of our commissioning editors will get in touch with you.

We're not just looking for published authors; if you have strong technical skills but no writing experience, our experienced editors can help you develop a writing career, or simply get some additional reward for your expertise.

Nginx HTTP Server

ISBN: 978-1-849510-86-8   Paperback: 348 pages

Adopt Nginx for your web applications to make the most of your infrastructure and serve pages faster than ever

1. Get started with Nginx to serve websites faster and safer

2. Learn to configure your servers and virtual hosts efficiently

3. Set up Nginx to work with PHP and other applications via FastCGI

4. Explore possible interactions between Nginx and Apache to get the best of both worlds

Squid Proxy Server 3.1: Beginner's Guide

ISBN: 978-1-849513-90-6   Paperback: 332 pages

Improve the performance of your network using the caching and access control capabilities of Squid

1. Get the most out of your network connection by customizing Squid's access control lists and helpers

2. Set up and configure Squid to get your website working quicker and more efficiently

3. No previous knowledge of Squid or proxy servers is required

Please check **www.PacktPub.com** for information on our titles

7412033R00131

Printed in Great Britain
by Amazon.co.uk, Ltd.,
Marston Gate.